United

FA CARLING PREMIERSHIP CHAMPIONS 1997

£5.50

Story of the Season 96-97

> What a wicked season it was. From Beckham's blindin' 50-yarder to Cantona's controversial decision to quit, there was never a dull moment. And it all began here....

AUGUST

⚽ PFA Young Player Of The Year David Beckham's half-way line howitzer against Wimbledon is tipped as goal-of-the-season as United go 10-11 favourites for the title....after only one game!

⚽ Fab Ravanelli bagged a hat-trick against Liverpool. Everton's 2 - 0 Goodison victory over Newcastle whets the appetite of future UEFA opponents, exposing the Brown-alers sieve-like defence.

⚽ Arsenal and Bruce Rioch part company as Gallic maestro Arsene Wenger gets set to usher in a new era at Highbury. The 'gaffer train' sees Kenny Dalglish departing Blackburn as Director of Football, while Terry Venables arrives at Portsmouth.

⚽ England prepare for the unknown; under Glenn Hoddle and against Moldova in a World Cup qualifier that sees Southhampton's Matt Le Tissier back in the squad.

⚽ Gianluca Vialli opens his Stamford Bridge account as the 'pasta master', under Ruud Gullit, puts Coventry to the sword with French freshman Frank Leboeuf completing the continental recipe for success.

⚽ Euro '96 hero Alan Shearer's first season for Newcastle starts miserably as Man.United sound an ominous warning - destroying The Magpies 4-0 in the Charity Shield at Wembley.

Managers in and out

● Bruce Rioch sacked by Arsenal.
● Ray Clemence leaves Barnet to become England goalkeeping coach.
● Sammy Chung sacked by Doncaster.
● Kerry Dixon becomes player/coach at Doncaster.
● Alan Ball resigns at Manchester City.

ON THE MOVE

PLAYER	TO	FROM	FEE
Paul Gerrard	Everton	Oldham	£1.5m
Jaime Moreno	Wash.DC	Middlesbrough	£100,000
Chris Day	Crystal Palace	Tottenham	£225,000
Richard Dryden	Southampton	Bristol City	£150,000
Anthony Barness	Charlton	Chelsea	£165,000
Bruce Grobbelaar	Plymouth	Southampton	Free
Wayne Collins	Sheffield Wed	Crewe	£650,000
Paul Parker	Derby	Man Utd	Free
Karel Poborsky	Man Utd	Slavia Prague	£3.5m
Jordi Cruyff	Man Utd	Barcelona	£800,000
Regis Genaux	Coventry	Stand. Liege	£1m
Espen Baardsen	Tottenham	SF Blackhawks	Free
Lee Sharpe	Leeds	Man Utd	£4.5m
Graham Potter	Stoke	Southampton	£250,000
Sasa Curcic	Aston Villa	Bolton	£4m
Patrick Vieira	Arsenal	AC Milan	£3.5m
Remi Garde	Arsenal	Strasbourg	Free
Niall Quinn	Sunderland	Man City	£1.3m
Kasey Keller	Leicester	Millwall	£900,000
Spencer Prior	Leicester	Norwich	£600,000
Patrik Berger	Liverpool	Bor.Dortmund	£3.5m
Paul Dickov	Man City	Arsenal	£750,000
Scott Canham	Brentford	West Ham	£25,000
Robbie Slater	Southampton	West Ham	£250,000
Ian Marshall	Leicester	Ipswich	£800,000

Story of the Season 96-97

England get it right in Moldova (where?) and Man.United do the same in Vienna, but Villa and Arsenal crash out of Europe – bah! Here's what else went on that month...

SEPTEMBER

⚽ Goals from super-captain Alan Shearer, Paul Gascoigne and Nicky Barmby see England cruise to an unspectacular 3-0 World Cup qualifying victory on a lethal Moldovan pitch. Scotland are held 0-0 against Austria.

⚽ Czech wizard Karel Poborsky gets a rare outing in Man Utd's 4-0 drubbing of Leeds, Wimbledon do the same to Everton and Middlesborough also grab a fab four against Coventry on the same Saturday.

⚽ Howard Wilkinson clears his desk at Elland Road. The vacancy is filled 24 hours later by former Gunners boss George Graham, after a year-long ban courtesy of the infamous bung scandal

⚽ The ghost of Bill Shankly, scissors in hand, is seen wandering around Anfield, the night after an Alice-banded Czech by the name of Patrik Berger slots a double on his full home debut, part of the 3-1 rout of Chelsea.

⚽ Bobby Gould leaves Ian Rush out of the Welsh squad, Gary Lineker accuses Vinnie Jones of being a "self hyped personality". Jones responds with the famous "jellyfish" tag. Round One to Vinnie.

⚽ Arsenal's in-form midfield star Paul Merson is rewarded for his courage when, 22 months after publicly admitting to his drink, drugs and gambling addictions, he receives a recall to the England squad for the World Cup qualifier against Poland at Wembley.

⚽ Bruce Rioch (right) is installed alongside QPR boss Stewart Houston as the Loftus Road No.2, and Kenny Dalglish resists Chairman Franny Lee's offer to join Man City.

⚽ The road to European glory begins. Villa go out of the UEFA on away goals to Helsingsborgs and Arsenal follow suit, the wrong side of a 6-4 marathon with German Bundesliga side Borussia Moenchengladbach. But Newcastle and Man United both record victories, against Halmstaad and Rapid Vienna respectively to keep the flag flying.

Managers in and out

- Ray Wilkins resigns at QPR.
- Howard Wilkinson sacked by Leeds.
- George Graham takes over.
- Stewart Houston takes over at QPR.
- Archie Gemmill and John McGovern leave Rotherham by mutual consent.
- Danny Bergara joins Rotherham.
- Alan Smith released by Wycombe Wanderers.

ON THE MOVE

PLAYER	TO	FROM	FEE
Paul Gerrard	Everton	Oldham	£1.5m
Andy Turner	Portsmouth	Tottenham	£250,000
Claus Lundekvam	Southampton	SK Brann	£400,000
Chris Waddle	Falkirk	Sheff Wed	Free
Gerard McMahon	Stoke	Tottenham	£450,000
Gary Elkins	Swindon	Wimbledon	£80,000

> Red nosed Devil Peter Schmeichel's faces goes as red as his beak following another couple of clangers...but there's more England joy at Wembley. Absolutely Wicked!

OCTOBER

Benito Carbone, Sheffield Wednesday's £4.5 million signing from Inter, proves no help in the 4-2 defeat at Wimbledon - making it six wins in a row and fifth place in the table for The Dons..

Man Utd's Peter Schmeichel suffers the recurring nightmare of footballs whistling past his nose thanks to a sensational 5- 0 pasting by Newcastle. A week later and United lose 6-3 at Southampton.

Naughty boys out in force. Villa keeper Mark Bosnich is charged by the FA over an alleged 'Nazi' salute at Tottenham. Paul Gascoigne admits to assaulting his wife Sheryl and Faustino Asprilla goes AWOL from training at Newcastle.

More World Cup success for England, beating Poland 2-1 at Wembley, shortly before the Venue of Legends gets the vote as the home for the new national stadium. Scotland win 2-0 in Latvia, Wales go down 3-1 to Holland and N. Ireland draw 1-1 with Albania.

Coventry and Southampton get that sinking feeling after a 1-1 draw and prepare to make camp at the bottom of the table. Could they both possibly escape from this?

The great Europe debate continues: Man Utd lose 1-0 away to Champions League rivals Fenerbahce, Newcastle see off Ferencvaros 6-3 and Liverpool tot up an 8- 4 scoreline against Sion.

George Graham's returns to Highbury with Leeds, but without the skills of Swede Tomas Brolin, deciding that retirement is preferable to honouring his contract at the Yorkshire club.

The whole of football mourns the death of Chelsea backer Matthew Harding, tragically killed with three other friends in a helicopter crash following The Blues' Coca-Cola Cup defeat at Bolton.

Managers in and out

- Arsene Wenger takes charge at Arsenal.
- Steve Parkin takes over at Mansfield after spell as caretaker manager.
- Steve Coppell leaves post as Technical Director at Palace to become Man City boss.
- Phil Neal leaves Cardiff to become Man City No.2.
- Ray Harford resigned at Blackburn.
- Pat Holland is sacked by Leyton Orient.

ON THE MOVE

PLAYER	TO	FROM	FEE
Eyal Berkovic	Southampton	Maccabi Haifa	£1m
Graham Kavanagh	Stoke	Middlesbrough	£750,000
John Hendrie	Barnsley	Middlesbrough	£250,000
Paul McGrath	Derby	Aston Villa	£200,000
Benito Carbone	Sheffield Wed	Inter Milan	£2.6m
Ulrich Van Gobbel	Southampton	Galatasaray	£1.3m
Darren Williams	York	Sunderland	£50,000
Neil Shipperley	Crystal Palace	Southampton	£1m
Eddie McGoldrick	Man City	Arsenal	£312,000
Adrian Whitbread	Portsmouth	West Ham	£200,000
Nick Barmby	Everton	Middlesbrough	£5.75m

Story of the Season 96-97

El Tel's been taken to Oz and Aussie Mark Bosnich has been taken to the cleaners – he got fined a thousand quid for his very poor impression of Adolf Hitler.

NOVEMBER

Blackburn Rovers turn back the clock by giving Liverpool a 3-0 tonking at Ewood Park. Gordon Strachan takes over from Big Ron at Coventry.

Ice-cool Arsene Wenger sings the praises of red hot goal maestro Ian Wright after his double Coca-Cola strike against Stoke paves the way for a 5-2 thriller. The dour looking Frenchman nearly breaks into a smile when the Gunners beat Spurs in the North London derby.

Man.United don't know whether to laugh or cry. They beat Arsenal in a top of the table clash but Juventus are on hand with a 1-0 Champions' League defeat days later, popping the Old Trafford balloon despite a second half charge.

Dennis Bergkamp (right) and his Dutch buddies lead Wales a merry dance (seven times to be precise), England keep Georgia off their minds with a 2-0 away win and a John McGinlay goal sees Scotland beat Sweden at Ibrox.

Terry Venables sets out to advance Australia's football fare when he agrees to coach the 'Socceroos', including Villa's Mark Bosnich, £1,000 worse off after the FA reach a decision on the now infamous 'Nazi' salute incident.

Brazilian Emerson (left) also upsets his accountant as he is fined £16, 000 after arriving late for

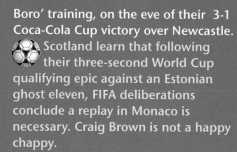

Boro' training, on the eve of their 3-1 Coca-Cola Cup victory over Newcastle.

Scotland learn that following their three-second World Cup qualifying epic against an Estonian ghost eleven, FIFA deliberations conclude a replay in Monaco is necessary. Craig Brown is not a happy chappy.

ON THE MOVE

PLAYER	TO	FROM	FEE
David Hillier	Portsmouth	Arsenal	£250,000
Gianfranco Zola	Chelsea	Parma	£4.5m
Scott Mean	West Ham	Bournemouth	Undisclosed
Peter Holcroft	Swindon	Everton	Free
John Spencer	QPR	Chelsea	£2.5m
Darren Huckerby	Coventry	Newcastle	£1m
Jason Cundy	Ipswich	Tottenham	£200,000
Neil Heaney	Man City	Southampton	£500,000
Jamie Pollock	Bolton	Middlesbrough	£1.5m
Frankie Bennett	Bristol Rovers	Southampton	£15,000
Jason Kavanagh	Wycombe	Stoke	£20,000
Steffen Iversen	Tottenham	Rosenborg	£2.7m
Phil Charnock	Crewe	Liverpool	Undisclosed

Managers in and out

- Brian Laws is sacked by Grimsby. Keith Houchen is dismissed by Hartlepool.
- John Gregory takes over at Wycombe.
- Ron Atkinson moves to post of Director of Football at Coventry.
- Gordon Strachan takes over at Coventry.
- Tommy Taylor leaves Cambridge to take over at Leyton Orient.
- Jim Platt sacked by Darlington.
- Steve Coppell resigns at Man City.
- Russell Osman joins Cardiff.
- Roy McFarland takes over at Cambridge.
- David Hodgson joins Darlington.

The man being hailed as 'the new Klinsmann' arrives at White Hart Lane and Frank Clark (right) takes the job nobody wanted...boss of Manchester City. Check it out......

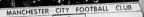
MANCHESTER CITY FOOTBALL CLUB

DECEMBER

Sheffield Wednesday defender Peter Atherton follows Steve McManaman around Anfield like cheap aftershave as the Merseysiders go down 1-0 at home, prompting accusations that they are over-reliant on their England magician.

Third round draw for the FA Cup sees two, all-Premiership ties with Sunderland's visit to Highbury looking like a day in the park compared to Spurs' trip to Old Trafford. The Roker men prepare for their London visit with a 3-0 win over Chelsea, the first time they have scored three goals for seven months.

The spaghetti-legs of Faustino Asprilla manage two goals in as many minutes, before the Colombian is stretchered off, as the Magpies put two past Metz to secure their place in the next round of the UEFA Cup. Man.United beat Rapid Vienna 2-1 away.

Problematic Romanian Florin Raducioiu plays his part in the Hammers comeback as they earn a 2-2 draw at home to Man Utd. The Red Devils make amends with a 5-0 thrashing of Sunderland.

The £2.6 million arrival of Steffen Iversen turns White Hart into Memory Lane as the Jurgen Klinsmann lookalike boosts hopes of a revival. Iversen's first goal for the club in the 3-1 win over Southampton provides some seasonal cheer, although Iversen insists he is no Jurgen. Days later Spurs are embarrassingly stuffed 7-1 by Newcastle.

Sven Goran Eriksson, Sampdoria's Swedish coach agrees to take over at Blackburn though he's unable to commit himself until the following summer. Tony Parkes continues as the reluctant caretaker manager.

£8.5 million former City Ground favourite Stan Collymore nets two in Liverpool's 4-2 demolition of Forest. Captain Stuart Pearce prepares for the thankless task of keeping his team up.

Frank Clark signs up for the most cursed job in football when he agrees to become manager of Manchester City. Chairman Frannie Lee heaves a sigh of relief after being snubbed by all and sundry. City fans are still looking at the play-offs but avoiding the drop is Frank's priority.

Managers in and out

- Jimmy Case is sacked by Brighton.
- Steve Gritt takes over at Brighton.
- Frank Clark resigns at Forest.
- Steve Thompson is sacked by Notts County.
- Kenny Swain takes charge at Grimsby.
- Mick Tait takes over at Hartlepool.
- Frank Clark takes charge at Man.City.

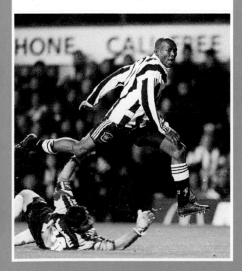

ON THE MOVE

PLAYER	TO	FROM	FEE
John Scales	Tottenham	Liverpool	£2.6m
Gunner Halle	Leeds	Oldham	£475,000
Matt Jackson	Norwich	Everton	£450,000
Gavin Peacock	QPR	Chelsea	£800,000
John Sheridan	Bolton	Sheff Wed	£180,000
Terry Phelan	Everton	Chelsea	£850,000

Story of the Season 96-97

King Kev goes, King Kenny comes in and it's mayhem on Tyneside – but things could be worse....especially if you're West Ham, Vialli or Ravanelli.

JANUARY

⚽ Gianluca Vialli (above), unhappy at being left on the subs' bench at The Bridge, decides not to tear his hair out, choosing instead to fire two in Chelsea's superb 4-2 FA Cup comeback after being two down against Liverpool.

⚽ Kevin Keegan vehemently denies resigning before Newcastle's 7-1 defeat of Tottenham. A week later he quits as Magpies boss. Kenny Dalglish is named as his successor.

⚽ West Ham fans take their FA Cup defeat by giant-killing Wrexham badly, invading the pitch to express their dissatisfaction.

⚽ Arsenal put Sunderland out of the FA Cup in a replay then try to sign Paris St Germain's 17-year-old wonderboy Nicolas Anelka. They're also linked with the De Boer brothers, Frank and Ronald, from Ajax as new manager Arsene Wenger continues his Euro search for new players.

⚽ Everton's slide to the relegation zone accelerates with a 4-1 defeat by Newcastle soon after a 3-2 FA Cup Fourth Round exit against First Division strugglers Bradford City (below).

⚽ Bryan Robson's Boro' are deducted three points for cancelling their December fixture against Blackburn (how fatal will that prove?). Fabrizio Ravanelli is later quoted as saying his move to Teesside was a mistake and Middlesbrough are destined to go down.

⚽ Blackburn full-back Graeme Le Saux enjoys a recall to the England squad, a year after dislocating an ankle and breaking a fibula in a mistimed tackle on Middlesborough's Juninho.

ON THE MOVE

PLAYER	TO	FROM	FEE
Maik Taylor	Southampton	Barnet	£500,000
Ramon Vega	Tottenham	Cagliari	£3.75m
Robert Molenaar	Leeds	FC Volendam	£1m
Ilie Dumitrescu	Club de Futbol	West Ham	£1m
Jan Eriksson	Sunderland	Helsingborgs	£250,000
Florin Raduciou	Espanol	West Ham	£2.5m
Gordon Watson	Bradford	Souhampton	£550,000
Claus Thomsen	Everton	Ipswich	£900,000
Matt Elliott	Leicester	Oxford	£1.6m
Paul Read	Wycombe	Arsenal	£35,000
Andy Linighan	Crystal Palace	Arsenal	£100,000
Anders Limpar	Birmingham	Everton	£100,000
Andre Kanchelskis	Fiorentina	Everton	£8m
Gary Breen	Coventry	Birmingham	£2.5m
Alex Evtushok	Coventry	D.Dnepropetrovsk	£800,000
Jan Age Fjortoft	Sheff Utd	Middlesbrough	£700,000
Gianluca Festa	Middlesbrough	Inter Milan	£2.7m
Vladimir Kinder	Middlesbrough	Slovan Bratislava	£1.3m

Managers in and out
- Kevin Keegan resigns at Newcastle.
- Kenny Dalglish replaces Keegan at Newcastle.
- Sam Allardyce joins Notts County.
- Alan Buckley sacked by West Brom.

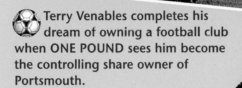

> It's double agony for 15 million pound man Alan Shearer, as England go down to a Zola goal at Wembley and he's then ruled out for six weeks with injury.

FEBRUARY

England repeat Man.United's brace of 1-0 defeats to Italian opposition with their defence alarmingly rusty under examination from Cesare Maldini's Azurri. On the day England launch their bid for the 2006 World Cup, Gianfranco Zola turns party pooper with a well-taken goal.

The Scotland and Estonia farce ends in a dreary 0-0 in Monaco, as does the clash at Cardiff Arms Park between Wales and the Republic of Ireland. Northern Ireland win 3-0 against Belgium.

Tottenham are left wondering just what they have to do to beat West Ham after a Julian Dicks penalty eventually gives The Hammers a 4-3 win. Dicks pays tribute to Spurs' skipper David Howells who turns out despite the death of his father 48 hours earlier.

Man United step up their title bid with a 2-1 win at Highbury. The match is remembered for Ian Wright's over tackle on Peter Schmeichel which Wright follows up with claims of racist abuse from the United keeper.

Terry Venables completes his dream of owning a football club when ONE POUND sees him become the controlling share owner of Portsmouth.

Managers in and out
- Neil Warnock sacked by Plymouth.
- Ray Harford takes charge at West Brom.
- Jiimmy Nicholl sacked by Millwall.
- John Docherty takes over at Millwall for the second time.
- Graham Sharp resigns from Oldham.
- Mick Buxton leaves Scunthorpe by mutual consent.
- Brian Laws joins Scunthorpe.
- Neil Warnock takes charge at Oldham.
- Dave Bassett leaves Crystal Palace to become Nottingham Forest's General Manager.

Crewe deny reports that a newly formed 'alliance' with Liverpool means they are now a nursery club for Anfield.

A goal from Brazilian ace Juninho puts troubled Manchester City out of the FA Cup, whilst 10 years after Keith Houchen's goal gave them victory at Wembley, Coventry put paid to Blackburn's hopes with a 2-1 win.

Alan Shearer's season continues to peak and trough as he misses six matches, including the UEFA Cup tie against Monaco, the result of his third groin operation since the previous April.

ON THE MOVE

PLAYER	TO	FROM	FEE
Paul Kitson	West Ham	Newcastle	£2.3m
Steve Jones	Charlton	West Ham	£400,000
John Hartson	West Ham	Arsenal	£3.3m
Robert Ullathorne	Leicester	Osasuna	£600,000
Per Pedersen	Blackburn	Odense	£2.5m
Mark Schwarzer	Middlesbrough	Bradford	£1.5m
John Ebbrell	Sheff Utd	Everton	£1m
Steve Guppy	Leicester	Port Vale	£850,000
Paul Beesley	Man City	Leeds	£500,000
Kevin Scott	Norwich	Tottenham	£250,000

Story of the Season 96-97

What a month for top soccer. United polish off Porto and Newcastle and Liverpool produce the game of the season – a 4-3 epic at Anfield.

MARCH

⚽ Manchester United turn on the style in a 4-0 rout of FC Porto in the Champions' League. Andy Cole gives a virtuoso performance then adds a goal to those of Giggs, May (above) and Cantona as United head for the semis.

⚽ Robbie Fowler shows dazzling skill to score an away-leg blinder in Liverpool's 3-1 aggregate win over Norwegians Brann Bergen in the Cup Winner's Cup, while Newcastle fall victim to the class of Monaco, departing the UEFA Cup on the wrong end of a 4-0 aggregate hiding.

⚽ Liverpool keep the spotlight shining brightly on Merseyside when they renew their tussle with the muscle of Newcastle's gladiators, for a repeat of last season's 4-3 epic. A very late goal from Robbie Fowler means there are no complaints at Anfield.

⚽ Steffen Iversen gives the Spurs faithful something to smile about by hitting a hat-trick against Southampton. Arsenal notch up a 2-0 win against Everton before doing the

same to Nottingham Forest.

⚽ England coach Glenn Hoddle dismisses a rift between himself and Alex Ferguson as the Manchester United boss threatens to refuse to release his players for the England friendly against Mexico.

⚽ Derby crash 6-1 to Middlesbrough in the League and their hopes of revenge in the FA Cup are dashed as Ravanelli, hat-trick hero in the first meeting, nets again in the 2-0 win two days later.

Managers in and out

● Joe Jordan leaves Bristol City by mutual consent.
● John Ward takes charge at Bristol City.
● Joe Royle leaves Everton by mutual consent.
● Alan Mullery stands down to focus on original role as club scout at Barnet.
● Terry Bullivant takes over first team duties at Barnet.

ON THE MOVE

PLAYER	TO	FROM	FEE
Micky Evans	Southampton	Plymouth	£600,000
Tommy Wright	Man City	Nott'm Forest	£450,000
Nicolas Anelka	Arsenal	Paris St Germain	£500,000
Pierre Van Hooijdonk	Nott'm Forest	Celtic	£4.5m
Ian Moore	Nott'm Forest	Tranmere	£1m
Paul Hyde	Leyton Orient	Leicester	Non-Contract
Kim Heiselborg	Sunderland	Esberg	£125,000
Danny Granville	Chelsea	Cambridge	£300,000
Alex Massinger	Arsenal	Cazino Graz	£400,000
Phil King	Swindon	Aston Villa	Free
Jorgen Nielsen	Liverpool	Hvidovre	£400,000
Carl Tiler	Sheff Utd	Aston Villa	£650,000
Mart Poom	Derby	Flora of Tallin	£500,000
Mark Tinkler	York	Leeds	£75,000
Paulo Wanchope	Derby	Herediano	Combined fee
Mauricio Solis	Derby	Heredianoof	£1.2m
Pierre Laurent	Leeds	Bastia	£500,000
Steve Lomas	West Ham	Man City	£1.6m
Des Hamilton	Newcastle	Bradford	£1.5m
David Billington	Sheff Wed	Peterborough	£500,000
Alan Miller	West Brom	Middlesbrough	£500,000
Steve Morrow	QPR	Arsenal	£500,000
Derek Lilley	Leeds	Greenock Morton	£500,000
Keith O'Halloran	St Johnstone	Middlesbrough	£50,000

Story of the Season 96-97

Just when Middlesbrough thought they were on the glory trail, up popped Heskey, then Claridge and a bunch of nobodies from Chesterfield to wreck the Boro dream.

APRIL

Bryan Robson experiences the agony and the ecstasy as Fabrizio Ravanelli's 95th minute extra time Coca-Cola Cup final strike is cancelled out by Leicester's Emile Heskey, two minutes from the end. Steve Claridge's extra-time strike in the Hillsborough replay takes the Foxes into Europe.

Italy and Poland's goal-less draw means England may qualify for France '98 without the trauma of play-offs. Northern Ireland suffer a 2-1 defeat at the hands, or feet, of Ukraine as the Republic go down 3-2 to Macedonia. Scotand see off Austria 2-0 thanks to rejuvenated Kevin Gallacher's first goals for Scotland in three and a half years.

Things are proving tense at the top: Arsenal manager Arsene Wenger pours scorn on Alex Ferguson's appeals to extend the season as his battle-weary troops surrender 1-0 in the first leg of their Champions League semi-final away to Borussia Dortmund. Days later United are caught napping at home, buckling 3-2 to Derby.

In one of the last matches to be played in the Parc des Princes, Paris St Germain extinguish Liverpool's UEFA hopes in a miserable evening for David James and Co. A 3-0 deficit looks an impossible mountain to climb at Anfield.

Boro's marathon Cup run hits 'the wall' as a strike from Chesterfield's Jamie Hewitt, again two minutes from the end of extra time, helps the dreaming Spireites to a 3-3 draw and an FA Cup semi-final replay after an absolute classic.

In the other semi-final, London neighbours Chelsea derail Wimbledon's outstanding season after two Mark Hughes goals and a gem from Gianfranco Zola ensure Joe Kinnear has plenty to shout about in the Dons changing room.

Man Utd keep cool when the heat is on thanks to an unlikely pair from Old Trafford old-timer Gary Pallister in the 3-1 win over Liverpool at Anfield. Five points clear and a game in hand, United look set to stay on top, as Arsenal manage only a 1-1 draw in an ill-tempered scuffle with Blackurn.

Bolton's 2-1 defeat of Manchester City is the cherry on the cake as they rise back to the Premiership next season. Alan Shearer becomes the PFA Player of the Year, with David Beckham taking the Young Player of the Year award. Emile Heskey proves he is one to watch as runner-up to the Leytonstone lad.

Wimbledon top The Fair Play League with 34 bookings and only one sending off in the season so far. At the other end of the chart, the Gunners are the naughty boys of the season with a total of 72 bookings and four sent off.

Managers in and out

● Danny Bergara sacked by Rotherham

ON THE MOVE

PLAYER	TO	FROM	FEE
Celestine Babayara	Anderlecht	Chelsea	£2.25m
Jan Dahl Thomasson	Heerenveen	Newcastle	£2.25m
Nick Weaver	Mansfield	Man.City	£200,000
Gustavo Payet	Real Zaragoza	Chelsea	FREE

A memorable and magnificent season comes to an end with Man.United celebrating another title success and Chelsea re-discovering the midas touch.

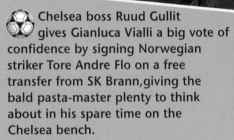

MAY

⚽ England revive their World Cup dreams with a workman-like 2-0 win over Georgia at Wembley. The ever-reliable SAS, Shearer and Sheringham, are on target as Glenn Hoddle's men shackle the tricky Georgians to close the gap on Italy in Group Two.

⚽ Everton's season goes from bad to worse when Bobby Robson unsurprisingly decides to bask in the Barcelona sun a little longer and rejects a move to Merseyside's crisis club. Skipper Dave Watson is still in temporary charge.

⚽ Chelsea boss Ruud Gullit gives Gianluca Vialli a big vote of confidence by signing Norwegian striker Tore Andre Flo on a free transfer from SK Brann, giving the bald pasta-master plenty to think about in his spare time on the Chelsea bench.

⚽ Manchester United don't even have to kick a ball to win the Premiership for the fourth time in five years as Liverpool show their infamous fighting spirit in a 2-1 defeat at Wimbledon. Commemorative T-shirts are available before the final whistle goes.

⚽ Stuart 'Psycho' Pearce hangs up his sheepskin coat and hands over managerial control to Dave Bassett as Forest contemplate another

⚽ Aston Villa part with £7 million for Brummie whinger Stan Collymore while former team-mate Robbie Fowler finishes as the season's top scorer with 31.

season of fun away days to Bury, Stockport and Swindon.

⚽ The final day of the season produces its usual mixture of celebration and misery. The area of most depression is the North East as Boro and Sunderland go down.

Managers in and out
- Fred Davies is sacked by Shrewsbury
- Mick Jones is appointed full-time manager at Plymouth.
- Billy Bonds is appointed Millwall boss.
- Jimmy Quinn and Mick Gooding leave Reading by mutual consent.
- Dave Bassett takes over as first team manager at Nott'm Forest from Stuart Pearce.
- Graham Taylor takes over as first team coach at Watford from Kenny Jackett who is appointed Taylor's number two
- Kenny Swain is sacked by Grimsby.
- Chris Nicholl resigns at Walsall.
- Jake King is appointed Shrewsbury manager.
- Gary Nelson resigns from Torquay.

ON THE MOVE

PLAYER	FROM	TO	FEE
Paul Emblen	Tonbridge Angels	Charlton	£7,500
Stan Collymore	Liverpool	A. Villa	£7m
David Robertson	Rangers	Leeds	£500,000
Slaven Bilic	West Ham	Everton	£4.5m
Matthew Rose	Arsenal	QPR	£500,000
Lee Hughes	Kidderminster	WBA	£200,000
Stefano Eranio	AC Milan	Derby	Free
Neil Cox	Middlesbrough	Bolton	£1.5m
Julian Darby	WBA	Preston	£150,000
Kevin Davies	Chesterfield	Southampton	£750,000
Clive Mendonca	Grimsby	Charlton	£700,000
Colin Murdoch	Man Utd	Preston	Free
Darren Wassall	Derby	Birmingham	unknown
Jonathon Hunt	Birmingham	Derby	£400,000
Dean Smith	Hereford	Orient	£42,500
Erik Nevland	V.Stavingar	Man Utd	unknown
Jason Lee	Nottm F.	Watford	£200,000
Lee Jones	Liverpool	Tranmere	£100,000

Beckham

Great goals

There have been many memorable goals scored over the last year and in this 'Great Goals' section we pay tribute to the men who produced moments of magic soccer fans will be talking about for years to come.

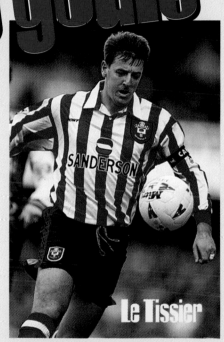
Le Tissier

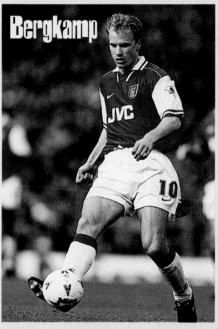
Bergkamp

Fowler

Zola

Shearer

Now turn over the page for special spotlights on the game's great goalscorers.

David Beckham

Man United & England

Great goals

What a fantastic couple of years it has been for DAVID BECKHAM. From being on the edge of stardom he suddenly plunged right in and has become one of the hottest properties in the game. Why? Just ask all the Premiership goalkeepers and they'll tell you why. Or, better still, ask the man himself.

Goal-den wonder: Becks cracks that goal against Wimbledon.

David Beckham

Beckham makes his England debut against Moldove.

 ## SO DAVE, TELL US ABOUT YOUR FAVOURITE GOAL.

I suppose the one against Wimbledon has to be my favourite, although there have been a few others that I have really enjoyed. I have a video of the goal against Wimbledon on the first day of last season and I still enjoy watching it. The goal was not an accident, I meant to do it in exactly the way that it went. I spotted the goalkeeper off his line and thought that I might as well have a go. I struck it well and it dipped at just the right moment. Afterwards, Neil Sullivan, the Dons goalkeeper congratulated me on a great goal. That was really nice of him.

 ## HAS YOUR EARLY SUCCESS BROUGHT ABOUT EXTRA PRESSURE?

It can be quite frightening to play in front of huge crowds, but part of being a pro is handling the pressure of being in front of thousands of people. I get a buzz from it now. It is the same off the pitch. I used to have a look at all the newspapers to see if I'd got a mention but since I have scored a few goals and played for England I get recognised all the time.

TALKING OF ENGLAND, HOW DO YOU ENJOY IT?

It's absolutely incred-ible. I don't think I'll ever experience anything like my England debut. It was away to Moldova and, having been called up by one of the greatest players of all time - Glenn Hoddle - I found myself among stars like Shearer, Gascoigne, Ince and Pearce, and I was amazed to be a part of it all.

BECAUSE YOU SCORE GREAT GOALS, DO PEOPLE NOW EXPECT YOU TO KEEP DOING IT?

The more you score, the more people expect you to score. It's actually got to the stage now where people urge me to shoot even when I'm way back in our half with the ball. I suppose the fact that very few of my goals have been tap-ins creates its own pressure. People start to expect you to do something even more spectacular than you have done before.

 ## WHAT IS IT LIKE WORKING WITH ALEX FERGUSON?

He has been brilliant, as he has with all the young players. His door is always open and he always finds time to talk if you need it. He expects you to work hard and do your best, but he doesn't expect miracles and he is very protective of his players.

 ## DO YOU EVER SEE YOURSELF LEAVING UNITED?

I love it here at United, and that is down to the fact that we have a great squad of players and a terrific manager. We also have the best of everything and we are successful. Old Trafford is a dream place to play and the supporters are tremen-dous. Where else would there be to go? It doesn't even enter my head.

Gianfranco Zola

Chelsea & Italy

He came, he saw, he conquered! The little man with the huge smile was the ace in the Chelsea pack last season and also proved that Italy cannot afford to leave him out of their World Cup battalion. His goal against England at Wembley was good; his goal for Chelsea in the FA Cup semis against Wimbledon was GREAT.

Great goals

Gianfranco Zola

Zola goala: Another beauty from Gianfranco.

DID YOU FIND A BIG DIFFERENCE BETWEEN ENGLISH AND ITALIAN FOOTBALL?

Yes, the styles are different and the players' attitudes are different. Also the climate! The Italian League is still regarded as the best but English football is not very far behind - and it is more interesting because there are so many different teams playing in different ways.

HOW FAR CAN CHELSEA GO?

All the way! Ruud Gullit is a very patient man who insists on good, entertaining football - that is his priority. He likes to win things too. He is still building his ideal squad and we are all still learning. Teams like Manchester United and Liverpool have been at the top longer - but we are fast catching up and I think that Chelsea can be champions soon.

HAVE YOU A FAVOURITE CHELSEA GOAL?

Most people seem to pick on the one I scored in the FA Cup semi-final against Wimbledon last season. I just got the ball, turned the Wimbledon defender, and sent the ball curling with my right foot. Everyone said it was a great goal but I was just happy that it went in and helped us to Wembley.

HOW DID YOU FEEL ABOUT SCORING AGAINST ENGLAND AT WEMBLEY?

Zola collects his Footballer of the Year award.

I felt very good because I had scored an important goal for my team against another team. I was doing my job. Afterwards I got a little good-natured stick from the English Chelsea players - and also just a little booing from a few opposition supporters - but that just shows how passionate they are for their national team, and that is good.

WILL YOU FINISH YOUR CAREER IN ENGLAND?

I have no idea. I haven't thought that far ahead. I like it at Chelsea and being in London - as long as I am happy and my family is happy then I will stay until I am no longer wanted. Who knows? That could be tomorrow - or maybe never. I am in no hurry to stop playing or to move somewhere else.

WHAT DID IT MEAN TO BE NAMED 'FOOTBALLER OF THE YEAR'?

It is difficult to explain. I could say fantastic, marvellous, wonderful - but they are not good enough words. It is something that I feel very deeply but cannot really express - except, perhaps, to say that I was very proud and happy to receive the award.

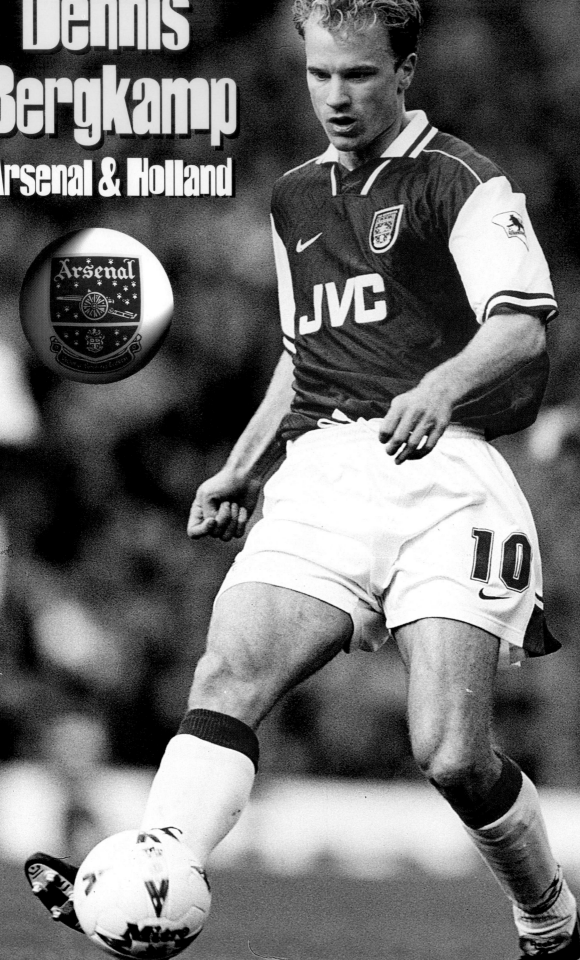

Dennis Bergkamp
Arsenal & Holland

Dennis Bergkamp

Great goals

Arsenal's season just got better and better in 96-97 - and so did Dennis Bergkamp. His goal against Sunderland at Highbury - a sublime piece of skill with a quality finish - summed up why the flying Dutchman is so important to the North Londoners. And he's going to get even better.

Dennis is a real Premiership menace.

WOULD YOU PREFER TO BE SCORING MORE GOALS?

Not necessarily! I have scored quite a few in my two full seasons at Highbury, and however many you get you always wish it was more. However, my role has been much more supportive to Ian Wright - or whoever else is the main striker - and if they are scoring freely then I am doing my job.

WHAT ABOUT THAT GREAT GOAL YOU SCORED AGAINST SUNDERLAND LAST SEASON?

You mean the FA Cup match at Roker Park! Yes, I was pleased with that one. I picked the ball up from a clearance, back-heeled it to create a space, then chipped it in a curve around their goal-keeper. It was a nice goal which excited a lot of people.

DO YOU FANCY HOLLAND'S CHANCES IN THE WORLD CUP?

Yes, I do! We have come through a difficult time which showed when we were unsuccessful in Euro'96, but we are better organised now and have put our troubles behind us. We have a good combination of young and experienced players and - especially with the World Cup being played in Europe - I think that we have a very good chance of success.

WHICH COUNTRY HAS THE BEST FOOTBALL - HOLLAND, ITALY OR ENGLAND?

England and Holland both have a much more attacking style than in Italy, which suits my play much better. There is not much to choose between England and Holland except that there are probably more big clubs in England - especially in the Premiership.

HAS YOUR TIME AT ARSENAL BEEN WHAT YOU HOPED?

Playing for Arsenal has been even better than I had dreamed. It took me a few

Bergkamp: Head and shoulders above the rest.

weeks to get used to the change of pace - because English football is much faster and more flexible than the Italian game that I had been playing for the previous two years. Once I'd settled down I loved every minute of it.

HAS ARSENE WENGER MADE MUCH DIFFERENCE?

Yes, he has changed things to his own style. He is a very experienced manager with a totally professional approach. His style has obviously suited us because our results and performances were greatly improved. He is a quiet man - but very determined.

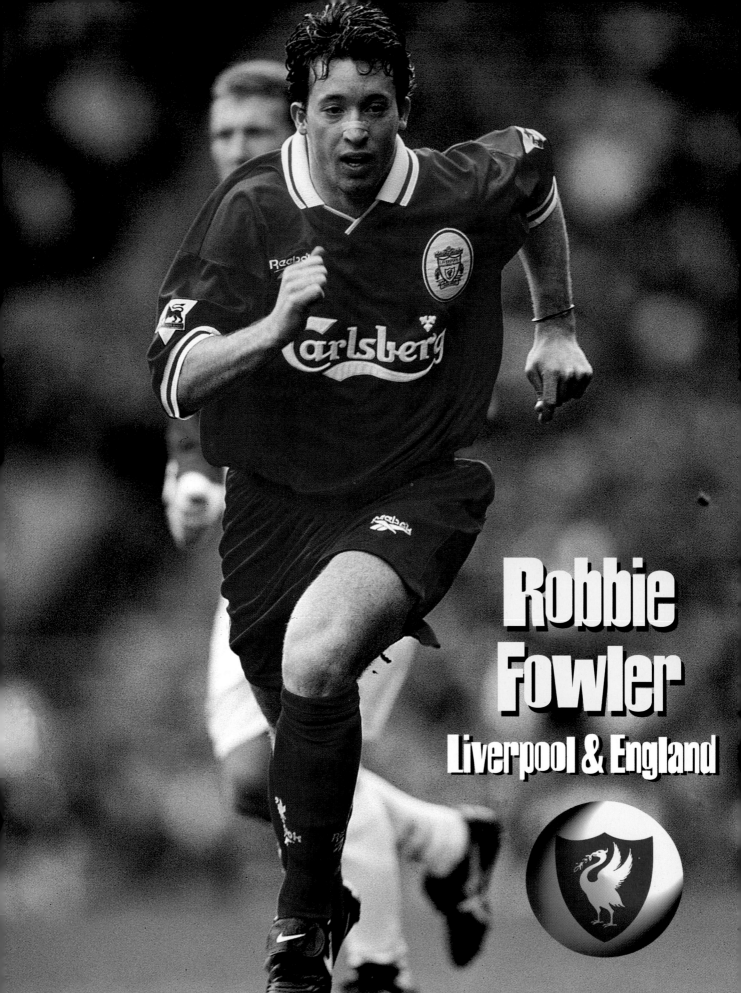

Robbie Fowler

Liverpool & England

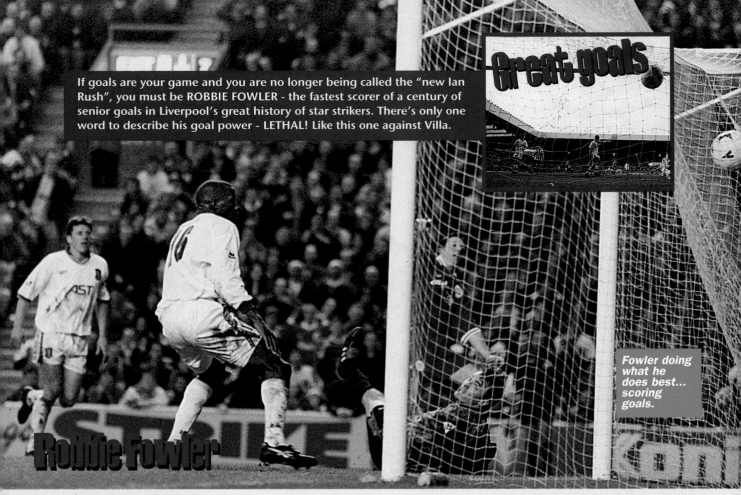

If goals are your game and you are no longer being called the "new Ian Rush", you must be ROBBIE FOWLER - the fastest scorer of a century of senior goals in Liverpool's great history of star strikers. There's only one word to describe his goal power - LETHAL! Like this one against Villa.

Robbie Fowler

Fowler doing what he does best... scoring goals.

HAS LIFE CHANGED MUCH SINCE YOU BECAME FAMOUS?

I'm earning a decent wage so that makes a difference to your lifestyle, but I'm still only Robbie Fowler the footballer and I don't think I've changed that much personally. I think my mates would say the same. I'm not as free to go about as much as I used to be because I get recognised a lot.

WHAT' IT LIKE BEING ON ON TV AND IN THE PRESS ALL THE TIME?

It makes me laugh when the media try to turn you into something that you are not. I've had journalists hanging around outside my house just in case there might be something to report. I think that's taking things a bit too far. At first I was bit put off by seeing my face everywhere but, after a while, you get used to it and you don't even notice.

YOU HAVE A BIT OF A REPUTATION AS A WILD BOY. IS THIS FAIR?

Not really. Well, I suppose that comes from liking a bit of a laugh. I enjoy joking about and sometimes that happens to be in public - like the famous sitting on the luggage conveyor belt at the airport. It's important for team spirit to laugh a lot, so I do my best to create some fun.

DOES SCORING GOALS EVER BECOME BORING

Robbie's a real model pro.

No way! I get a buzz every time I score, whether it's a simple tap-in or a real cracker. The feeling when the ball hits the back of the net and the crowd roars is like no other experience. It's fantastic and I never tire of it - I never will!

THAT WAS A CRACKER YOU GOT AGAINST ASTON VILLA LAST JANUARY!

It was very satisfying because I was in the right place at the right time - which is what my job is all about. Jamie Redknapp sent in a low, hard shot and Mark Bosnich couldn't hold it. I scooped the ball over him. Perhaps it wasn't brilliant but the things that we practice on the training ground instinctively happened - and that makes all the hard work really worth it.

DO YOU HAVE A FAVOURITE STRIKER?

I still rate Rushie - but the top man has to be Shearer. He is a perfect striker. I'm still trying to improve aspects of my game but he's got the lot. He could score goals for any team in the world. One day people will look back at his £15 million transfer and say it was a bargain.

Alan
Shearer
Newcastle
& England

Great goals

Alan Shearer, the man with the Midas touch, has scored so many wonder goals it's hard to single out one. But try the free-kick cracker against Leicester last season for starters...

Alan Shearer

Shearer in familiar pose... scoring for Newcastle.

HOW DO YOU FEEL ABOUT CAPTAINING ENGLAND?

I've won a few honours in the game and a few England caps as well, but captaining my country - and especially leading the team out at Wembley - is an honour above all others. It has given me my proudest moment.

WHAT IS IT LIKE HAVING KENNY DALGLISH AS MANAGER AGAIN?

He was the reason that I signed for Blackburn and we had three very good years together at Ewood Park. I was disappointed when Kevin Keegan left Newcastle because he was a great manager, but I was relieved and delighted when Kenny came here.

DO YOU FEEL THE PRESSURE TO SCORE?

There is always pressure in football, no matter what position you play.If you get a bit of a reputation everyone wants to play their very best against you, and the supporters expect you to respond. That is quite natural. The only other pressure is from the media if you haven't scored for a while - but I try to ignore that because it just doesn't help.

WHAT ABOUT THAT TERRIFIC FREE KICK AGAINST LEICESTER LAST SEASON?

I got a hat-trick that day and we won 4-3. The free-kick was the first. It was about 25 yards out and I put a bend on it as well as power. It certainly made the net bulge and the supporters went crazy. That's the sort of thing I practice when we are training.

DO YOU FANCY PLAYING ABROAD?

I know that there has been talk of me going to Italy - but it is only talk and it has been written about me for several years. It would seem a bit strange to be going abroad when so many top players are coming over here. I'm more than happy at Newcastle and I have no iimmediate plans to go abroad.

CAN NEWCASTLE WIN THE CHAMPIONSHIP?

Everyone has to do better than Manchester United. The team that does that will win the championship. We had a good run last season and finished second. A little more consistency and we might have finished at the top. Kenny achieved that when we were at Blackburn and I can see no reason why he shouldn't do it again with Newcastle.

Hands up if you're the best striker in Europe.

Matt
Le Tissier

Southampton
& England

Great goals

You can't beat a Matt finish to put a bit of gloss on an afternoon's soccer, especially when the Matt is Southampton's goal artist - LE TISSIER. The Saints maestro has created masterpiece after masterpiece - none better than the cracker he scored against Newcastle at The Dell last season.

Matt Le Tissier

WOULDN'T YOU LIKE TO MOVE TO ANOTHER CLUB?

"I have become a part of the furniture at the Dell and any talk of me leaving has only ever been just talk! I have never really wanted to leave Southampton, it is like home to me. Yes, it is flattering to know that other people are interested, but my plan has always been to stay with the Saints."

WOULD PLAYING FOR SOMEONE ELSE HAVE WON YOU MORE CAPS?

"I doubt that! I have surprisingly been picked for England when I haven't really been on my best form and, at other times, when I have felt good and been playing really well, I have been ignored. I'm not sure how it works."

WHAT'S THE SECRET OF YOUR SUPER GOALS?

"Not minding if I miss. You can only score goals by trying. Some players are put off by the reaction if they miss the target. That has never bothered me.

Matt - unsure where his England career is going.

Nobody has a go at me more than I do myself if I miss, but if you don't try to score then you never will!"

DO YOU FANCY ENGLAND'S WORLD CUP CHANCES?

"Yes, why not? I hope that I get the chance to play in a World Cup before I hang up my boots around the year 2003. Sometimes I think that we criticise ourselves too much. We have good players and we are still one of the teams all the other nations want to beat."

WHERE DID YOU BEGIN YOUR CAREER?

I was born in Guernsey in the Channel Islands and began playing for Vale Recreation. A Southampton scout spotted me and reported back to the Dell. I was invited to join the Saints as a junior and then they offered me a professional contract which I signed in October 1986.

WHAT HAS BEEN THE HIGHLIGHT OF YOUR CAREER?

There have been quite a few but, having gradually established myself in the Saints first team I was named PFA 'Young Player of the Year' in 1990 which was a great honour. Making my full international debut against Denmark in 1994 was another.

HOW DO YOU RELAX?

"Quietly! I like an evening at a nice restaurant with my wife, and I have even been known to play Bingo - anything that gets me away from it all! I like to read and I watch a bit of television - mostly comedy. I enjoy driving - my worst nightmare would be to wake up and find that I own a Robin Reliant!"

SHOOT QUIZ

Think you're a bit of a football boffin? Reckon you know all about players, matches, goals and grounds? Well, you've come to the right place to show off...or come a cropper! This is SHOOT's superb quiz section and we're out to get you...

Straight Outta The Blocks

Are you a fast starter? You'll have to be in Round One of our top footie quiz. You have TWO minutes to answer these 20 questions. Ready with the stopwatch? Go!

Season 1996-97

1. Who scored England's goals in the 2-0 World Cup qualifying win in Poland?

2. Who missed a penalty in that match?

3. Which Premiership team lost two Cup Finals in 1996-97?

4. Who's new home is called the Reebok Stadium?

5. Does Derby's Christian Dailly play for Wales, Northern Ireland or Scotland?

6. Which footballing minnows did Scotland struggle to beat 3-2 in a friendly in the summer of '97?

7. Eric Cantona was Manchester United's top scorer in 1996-97: true or false?

8. How many successive Premier Division titles have Rangers won?

9. Who scored Crystal Palace's winner in the 1997 First Division Play-Off Final?

10. Who was in goal when Chelsea won the 1997 FA Cup Final?

Summer Signings 1997

11. What country does Liverpool's purchase from Wimbledon, Oyvind Leonhardsen, play for?

12. How much did Sunderland pay Newcastle for Lee Clark; £1.5m, £2m or £2.5m?

13. Where did Jason Lee go to after leaving Nottingham Forest?

14. West Ham made a double signing for £3million in June 1997: one from QPR, one from Southampton. Who were they?

15. Aberdeen striker Scott Booth joined a Scottish team-mate at which German club?

16. Man United's first signing of the summer was Erik Nevland from Viking Stavanger in which country?

17. Rangers paid £4m for Lorenzo Amoruso from which Italian club?

18. Charlton broke their club transfer record to get which black-and-white stripped striker?

19. Who did Aston Villa pay £7 million for?

20. Emmanuel Petit and Gilles Grimandi both joined Arsenal for a combined £5 million from which French club?

All Quiz answers on page 35.

Where Am I?

Loads of teams are changing grounds and building new stadiums. But can you tell what grounds these are and who plays there?

1. Championship quality

2. The clue's in the colours

3. Wasps buzz around here

4. Tears on the Wear?

5. A river runs past it but there's no forest

6. Premiership action guaranteed every week

7. Pride of the Pennines, perhaps?

8. LFC: and it's not Lazio Football Club

9. It's in the city, definitely, maybe

10. All guns ablaze round here

The answers are on page 35.

1 and 2. These two got to know that Wembley winners feeling many more times after this one.

3. He's put on a few pounds since then...and made a few, wheeling and dealing in the East End. The boy done good too.

4. Recognise the Italian skills, calm tones and shiny head? Thought not.

5. He's still going in the Premiership, and in blue, with one England cap in the cupboard.

6. The hair's gone from bubble perm, to skinhead, to bleached blonde, to extensions and, finally, nearly nothing. But you must recognise this entertainer.

Those Were The Days

Blimey, are these dodgy old pics or what? Can you identify the current famous faces from years ago?

ANSWERS ON PAGE 35

9. The pop star looks, the shaggy hair, he's Mr Cool! Surely he must be a Gallagher or at least a Man City star? Not quite...

8. Who's this fresh-faced saintly youth? Well, he'd been through a bit since then...a few tackles in midfield, that is.

7. Back in the Midlands, this captain wasn't too marvellous and nearly fell through the trap door in '97.

10. With that blond mane, it must be Baby Spice! No, it's Leslie Ash! Not quite, but this chap sometimes behaved badly!

11. He's always been a bit of a menace and popped up at Wembley again to collect another winner's medal in May.

A Question

It's the famous BBC TV gameshow A Question of Sport...with a difference - it's all about the beautiful game. Get into two teams - you can have one, two, three or as many as you like in each team. Team A's questions are on the left page, Team B's on the right. Good luck!

Team A

Picture Board
Study the three pictures and see if you can tell who the mystery stars are.

Mystery Guest
Can you work out who the foreign superstar is who played in the Premiership in 1996-97 but looks more than comfortable behind the wheel?

What happened next?
It's the 1997 FA Cup Final and a cross flies into the Chelsea box from a Middlesbrough corner. But what happened next?

One Minute Round
You have 60 seconds to answer the following questions;
1. Where do Manchester City play their home games?
2. Name the Premiership's only father and son pair, one manager, one player.
3. What colour shirts do Plymouth wear?
4. Who are nicknamed The Bantams?
5. The following four players could all be found on the road. Use the clues to get their surnames.
Mark ——, Leeds motor
Steve ——r, Irish defender
Noel ——an, Sky Blue
Gary ——, Toffee-nose

Home or Away
Tackle the home question on a British club for one point or go away and try the question on a European one for two points.
Home: Who won the 1997 Auto Windscreens Shield - Crewe or Carlisle?
Away: Who won the 1997 Italian Cup - Vicenza or Roma?

# of Footie

Team B

Picture Board
Study the three pictures and see if you can tell who the mystery stars are.

Mystery Guest
Can you work out who the foreign superstar is who played in the Premiership in 1996-97 but has gone all hairy on us?

What happened next?
It's a big international on the road to France '98. But what on earth is going on?

Home or Away
Tackle the home question on a British player for one point or go away and try the question on a European one for two points.
Home: Which Man United and England defender is the youngest ever cricketer to play for Lancashire's second XI?
Away: Which country is Real Madrid's Roberto Carlos from?

One Minute Round
You have sixty seconds to answer the following questions;
1. Where do Sunderland play their home games?
2. Name the twin brothers: a defender at Sheffield United and a Wimbledon striker?
3. What colour shirts do Rotherham wear?
4. Who are nicknamed The Stags?
5. The following four players could all be found in the countryside. Use the clues to get their surnames.
Tim ———, the Rover

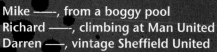

Mike ———, from a boggy pool
Richard ———, climbing at Man United
Darren ———, vintage Sheffield United

The Question of Footie answers are on page 35 - but no cheating! Don't look until you've finished the quiz

soccersearch

Hidden in the grid are the names of all twenty Premiership sides. Their names may be left to right, up or down or written diagonally. Can you find them?

W	H	Y	N	O	T	L	O	B	T	H	E	B	A	L	L
L	A	A	T	S	E	T	E	W	E	I	R	S	A	I	O
H	L	D	S	Y	G	N	V	E	U	V	T	N	B	V	E
W	E	S	T	H	A	M	L	A	D	A	E	G	O	E	D
O	S	E	C	R	E	T	K	O	W	S	L	R	A	R	R
T	V	N	P	O	S	M	Y	E	R	I	F	L	T	P	E
O	A	D	S	A	L	V	A	A	N	Y	S	E	B	O	M
T	S	E	C	K	E	B	E	N	B	U	O	I	S	O	N
T	A	W	A	S	H	A	N	R	U	B	K	C	A	L	B
E	E	F	W	R	C	T	E	D	Y	N	T	E	A	I	A
N	D	F	A	U	E	D	N	R	U	S	I	S	F	E	R
H	I	E	L	S	O	U	T	H	A	M	P	T	O	N	Z
A	R	H	C	T	B	N	H	A	N	I	Y	E	E	Y	S
M	E	S	W	A	E	T	D	U	B	V	T	R	G	D	L
A	L	L	I	V	N	O	T	S	A	R	S	G	M	S	E
R	E	N	O	D	E	L	B	M	I	W	A	L	T	E	Y
I	R	C	R	Y	S	T	A	L	P	A	L	A	C	E	P

The clubs are; Man United, Arsenal, Liverpool, Newcastle, Aston Villa, Chelsea, Sheff Wednesday, Wimbledon, Tottenham, Derby, Leeds, Everton, Blackburn, West Ham, Leicester, Coventry, Southampton, Bolton, Barnsley, Crystal Palace.

XWORD

Crossword grid (filled answers):
GIANFRANCOZOLA
NEVILLE · BARCELONA
LAJGE·DE·AGOSTINI
CASTLE · LAZIO · LEE
PETRIC · ADAMS
CANADA · REAL
METZ · IN NEAR · STAG
NEESKENS · TEL · JOHN
NADAL · TEAMMATE

answers

Straight Outta The Blocks Answers
Season 1996-97
1. Alan Shearer and Teddy Sheringham. 2. Shearer. 3. Middlesbrough. 4. Bolton Wanderers. 5. Scotland. 6. Malta. 7. False - it was Ole Gunnar Solskjaer. 8. Nine. 9. David Hopkin. 10. Frode Grodas.

Summer Signings
1. Norway. 2. £2.5m. 3. Watford. 4. Andrew Impey and Eyal Berkovic. 5. Borussia Dortmund. 6. Norway. 7. Fiorentina. 8. Clive Mendonca from Grimsby. 9. Stan Collymore from Liverpool. 10. Monaco.

A Question of Footie answers
Team A
Picture Board: 1. Jamie Redknapp. 2. David Hopkin. 3. Gary Pallister.
Mystery Guest: David Ginola.
What happened next? Gianluca Festa's header went in but was disallowed.
Home or Away: Home (1 pt) - Carlisle. Away (2 pts) - Vicenza.
One Minute Round: 1. Maine Road. 2. Harry and Jamie Redknapp. 3. Green and white stripes. 4. Bradford City. 5. Mark Ford, Steve Carr, Noel Whelan and Gary Speed.
Team B
Picture Board: 1. David Burrows. 2. Patrik Berger. 3. Steve Bull.
Mystery Guest: Gianluca Vialli.
What happened next? Scotland kicked off against no opposition as Estonia failed

to turn up. the game was abandoned after three seconds.
Home or Away: Home (1 pt) - Phil Neville. Away (2 pts) - Brazil.
One Minute Round: 1. Monkwearmouth Stadium. 2. David and Dean Holdsworth. 3. Red with white trim. 4. Mansfield Town. 5. Tim Flowers, Mike Marsh, Richard Trees, Darren Vine.

Where Am I? answers
1. Old Trafford, Manchester United. 2. Villa Park, Aston Villa. 3. Loftus Road, QPR. 4. Riverside Stadium, Middlesbrough. 5. City Ground, Nott'm Forest. 6. Selhurst Park, C.Palace and Wimbledon. 7. Ewood Park, Blackburn. 8. Anfield, Liverpool. 9. Maine Road, Manchester City. 10. Highbury, Arsenal.

Those Were The Days answers
1 and 2. Dave Watson and Steve Bruce. 3. Harry Redknapp. 4. Ray Wilkins. 5. Kevin Richardson. 6. Gazza. 7. Gary McAllister. 8. Andy Townsend. 9. Brian McClair. 10. Lee Chapman. 11.Dennis Wise.

soccersearch

(word search grid)

Across:
1. He's the current Footballer of the Year (10, 4)
10. Even I'll turn out for Manchester United - twice! (anag) (7)
11. Present holders of the European Cup Winners Cup (9)
12. Fulham goalie in a clanger (5)
13 and 14 across. Italian international - get a side in disarray (anag) (2,8)
16. A New Englishman's home, proverbially speaking, in the North-East (6)
17. Gazza's team before joining Rangers (5)
18. Former Charlton player who moved on to Newcastle and England (3)
20. I crept about with a Yugoslavian at Rangers (anag) (6)
22. Stalwart defender of Arsenal and England (5)
23. Mix clues up for Romanian international (anag) (7)
27. Goalie Craig Forrest plays for this country (6)
28 across and 6 down. Team that beat Arsenal in 1995 European Cup Winners Cup Final (4,6)
29. French club knocked out of UEFA Cup last season by Newcastle (4)
31. (see 38 down)
33. Creature on the Mansfield Town badge (4)
36. Ken's seen a Dutch star of the 70s (anag) (8)
37. Familiar name given to England's boss before Hoddle (3)
38. (See 32 down)
39. Land a new role with Barcelona and Spain (anag) (5)
40. He's on your side! (8)

Down:
1. Newcastle forward to be found in goal, perhaps (anag) (6)
2. Defender who spent 20 years at West Ham (5,6)
3. Street where the Coca-Cola Cup resides (7)
4. Scottish winners of 1983 European Cup Winners Cup (8)
5. Caribbean island that qualified for 1998 World Cup Finals (4)
6. (See 28 across)
7. Huddersfield's ground used to be called this and their new stadium is just off it (5,4)
8. Basile -, played for Rangers before moving to Monaco (4)
9. Grimsby man - or Paul, star of Ipswich and England in the early 80s (7)
15. Pat Nevin's first club who sold him down the river (5)
18. Malt bar for someone in Dortmund (anag) (7)
19. Nigel, who played for Chelsea, Liverpool and Rangers (8)
21. He managed to move from the City Ground to City's ground (5)
22. Aston Villa's Mark Bosnich plays for them (9)
24. A formulated way to play in Lapland! (4)
25. How to raise the money to buy a goalkeeper (4)
26. Does it show the referee's assistant is beginning to tire? (4)
30. Hibs defender who's obviously Scotland material (5)
32 down and 38 across. Liverpool and Scotland star of the sixties, now a TV pundit (3,2,4)
34. Has, by arrangement, played for Brentford (anag) (5)
35. The Scottish Coca-Cola Cup used to be called the - Cup (4)
37. The legendary Preston and England winger - Finney (3)
38 down and 31 across. Manager

Answers on page 125

STAN COLLYMORE
ASTON VILLA

All the money and glamour might be in the Premiership, but there's no shortage of excitement in the lower Leagues. The spotlight is firmly on the big clubs in the top flight, but when the focus is briefly switched, the Nationwide League rarely lets anyone down.

And last season was no exception as there was excitement at both ends of all three divisions right up until the last day of the season. After all, it doesn't get any more dramatic then Hereford meeting Brighton on the final day to determine which one would stay in the League.

Not even the race for the Premiership title could match the sheer drama and tension of that occasion. And there were other great tussles as well...the battle to avoid the drop from the First Division...and the battle to replace them from the Second. And once all that was done, there were still the play-offs to look forward to... play-offs which turned out to be among the most dramatic ever.

All in all, it was a memorable season in the Nationwide League and here we pay tribute to some of the teams and individuals who helped to make it so good...

Football League Extra

B the Best

Bolton Wander back into the big time

At the start of May 1996, Bolton were a club in turmoil having plunged out of the Premiership after just one season in the big time.

By May 1997, they were back in the top flight, seemingly bigger and better than ever.

Bolton turned the First Division Championship race into a cake-walk and, from Christmas onwards, there were never any doubts which side would take the title.

But it wasn't just the fact that they bounced back from the disappointment of relegation the previous year which made their achievement so special. It was the manner in which they achieved it

Quite simply, they destroyed the opposition and they came perilously close to achieving a fantastic double.

Going into the last game of the season against Tranmere they needed a win to reach 100 points, and two goals to notch 100 goals.

They got the two goals they needed, but had to settle for a 2-2 draw so finishing tantalisingly close to the magic ton on 98 points.

But no-one at Burnden Park was complaining and they regained their place among the mighty in the Premiership. This time, they'll be hoping to stay for a while longer.

Tyke that

Barnsley are set to party

When the pre-season promotion favourites were being discussed, it was teams like Wolves, Sheffield United and QPR that dominated the conversations. Very few people gave Barnsley too much hope of gatecrashing the Premiership party, but no-one told Danny Wilson and his team.

The former Luton and Sheffield Wednesday midfielder has moulded a classy side at Oakwell and their slick brand of passing football was good enough to earn them second place and a spot in the Premiership's promised land.

Typically, no sooner had they got there than people were predicting their demise, but Wilson was in no mood to listen to the detractors.

He insisted: "People wrote us off all last season but our tremendous camaraderie has taken us a long way.

"Football is not just about how much money you spend. Clubs like Wimbledon have survived in the top flight without splashing out millions of pounds and they must be an inspiration to us."

And you can be sure of one thing, no matter what Barnsley's fate, their fans will have a good time.

"It's just like watching Brazil," is their famous chant to their heroes and, while Juninho and Co might have something to say about that, there's no doubt Barnsley will surprise a few clubs this term.

The Key Men

Neil Redfearn

One of the best goalscoring midfielders in the game, Redfearn again passed the 15 goal tally last season. He's a been a regular on the scoresheet wherever he has played throughout his career, but in the last few seasons at Oakwell he has really come to the fore. Probably only his age - he's 32 - prevented a Premiership club snapping him up but now he'll get the chance to show what he can do on the biggest stage.

John Hendrie

Like Sellars at Bolton, Hendrie took something of a gamble when he quit Middlesbrough for Barnsley, but it's a gamble that paid off spectacularly. Because while Boro were battling against the drop - a fight they of course lost - Hendrie was riding high with his new team. His goals, and more importantly his experience, were vital as Barnsley held off the challenge of the chasing pack to clinch promotion.

The play-offs perfectly sum up the agony and ecstasy of football. For three teams, it's like winning the Lottery. For the others, it's like...well, forgetting to do the Lottery and seeing your numbers come up. But there have to be losers and, as we see here, there have to be winners...

Hip-Hop Hooray

David **Hopkin** fired Crystal Palace into the Premiership in a complete reversal of the 1996 First Division play-off Final at Wembley.

On that occasion, it was Palace who were left crying in their beer as Leicester beat them with a last-gasp goal from Steve Claridge.

But this year it was the Londoners doing the celebrating as they did exactly the same thing to Sheffield United.

There were just seconds remaining when Hopkin collected the ball 25 yards from goal...and curled a stunning winner into the top corner of Simon Tracey's net.

There was barely time for United to restart the game before the referee blew the whistle on their Premiership dream.

And that left Hopkin beaming: "That made it 17 goals for the season for me, but that was the most special because it came in the most important game of the campaign and at Wembley.

"When the ball first came to me I was going to cross it, but then I looked up and decided to curl it into the top corner.

"There was no way United could come back from that. The goal might be worth £10 million to the club but, for the players, the most important thing is playing in the Premiership."

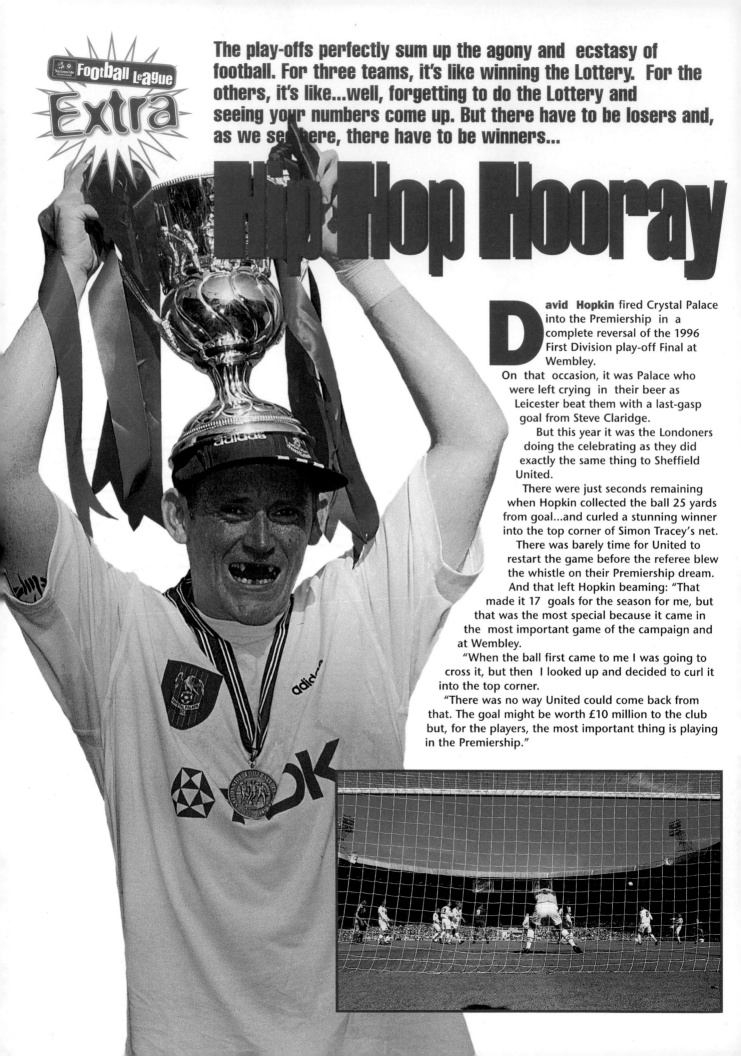

Rockin' Crewe

Shaun Smith was Crewe's hero as they booked their place in the First Division...for the first time this century!

It's 100 years since Alex last played at that level and it was a fitting reward for manager Dario Gradi's 14 years at the club.

They achieved their dream thanks to left-back Smith who drove the ball into the roof of the net for the only goal of the game to shatter Brentford.

Five years ago, Smith was playing non-League football for Emley. Next season he will be lining up against the like of Wolves, Manchester City and Middlesbrough.

He admitted: "I can't believe what has happened to me in the last five years, never mind winning and scoring at Wembley.

"We will try to stick together as a team and I think we are strong enough to hold our own in the First Division."

As for Gradi, he made it third time lucky after twice before losing at

Wembley - first as a player with non-League Sutton and then four years ago in the play-off Final against York.

He admitted: "The last time we were in the Play-off Final the players froze, but the game went for us this time.

"I've been confident we could get to the First Division. I just wasn't sure when."

Runaway Frain

John Frain fired Northampton into the Second Division in the most dramatic fashion possible.

The experienced full-back blasted a twice taken free-kick wide of Roger Freestone in the very last minute to send Northampton into raptures, and plunge Swansea into the depths of despair.

The Welshmen were furious after Frain's first free-kick was ordered to be re-taken because of encroachment.

And when he was given a second chance, Frain made no mistake as he curled his kick into the corner of the net.

It was Northampton's first trip to Wembley and manager Ian Atkins couldn't hide his delight at the outcome.

"The lads battled really hard to earn their

place at the Final and didn't let anyone down with their display on the day," he said.

"They can play better but I think we thoroughly deserved to win and all the lads will be able to look back on the day with a lot of satisfaction."

Nationwide PLAY-OFF WINNERS

Stockport bounty

Only the **most** hard-hearted of football fans would deny that Stockport deserved something from last season.

They captured the nation's hearts with a thrilling run to the Coca-Cola Cup Semi-Finals, a run which was only ended by Bryan Robson's foreign legion at Middlesbrough.

But it looked as though that Cup glory would ultimately cost them in the League as they slipped off the pace.

However, a tremendous late run, in which they won three of their last four games, saw County nick the second automatic promotion spot.

And as they proved in the Coke Cup last season, the better the opposition, the better they tend to play.

The Key Man

Alun Armstrong

When he was released by his home-town club Newcastle it must have felt like the end of the world for Armstrong. But he's proved at Stockport that he still has a very big future in the game. Still only 22, the lively striker is quick and skilful and always a handful for any defence. It seems only a matter of time before he's back at the top.

The Key Man

Warren Aspinall

Aspinall has had his problems in a somewhat chequered career, but he has proved to be an inspired signing for Carlisle. He's now 30 and appears to have cured some of his old ways which often saw him fall foul of referees and his own managers alike. But his experience has clearly helped a young Carlisle side to get back to Division Two.

Wigan cheer

Wigan's Division Three Championship triumph was just reward for chairman Dave Whelan's forward thinking and ambition.

Whelan opened himself up to ridicule by signing three Spaniards a couple of years ago, but the likes of Roberto Martinez and Isidro Diaz have proved to be tremendous assets.

And their Latin flair, coupled with a bit of good old northern grit, have proved to be an irresistible combination.

Wigan were riding high for much of the season and clinched the title on goal difference from Fulham with a last day victory over Mansfield.

And with Whelan prepared to put his money where his mouth is, this could be just the start for Wigan.

The Key Man

Graeme Jones

The Spaniards may have attracted most of the publicity down at Springfield Park, but there's no doubt who was the real star of last season. Striker Graeme Jones blasted 31 League goals - more than any other player in the country - to steer Wigan to the title. But whether The Latics will be able to fend off interest from bigger clubs is a big question.

Happy day

Carlisle bounced back from relegation in May 1996 to reclaim their place in the Second Division - and grabbed the Auto Windscreens Shield in the process.

That made it a memorable season for former West Ham goalkeeper Mervyn Day, who is now in charge at Brunton Park, and also for chairman Michael Knighton.

Knighton, a former Manchester United director, has ambitions to take Carlisle all the way to the Premiership and they are now heading back in the right direction.

And he, and Day, will be hoping that their stay in the Second Division lasts a bit longer than one season this time.

Unless of course they are heading for the First!

The Cumbrians got over the loss of top scorer David Reeves to Preston to clinch promotion with Allan Smart, who went from Deepdale to Brunton Park in the Reeves deal, grabbing vital goals along the way.

Ravin' Cottage

After ten years of almost non-stop misery, Fulham's fans finally had something to cheer about last season.

It was their first success for a decade and gave one of football's most well-known faces his greatest moment in football.

Fulham's chairman last term was BBC TV pundit Jimmy Hill and he reckoned that last year's success was just about his most memorable in his long association with the club.

Hill is no longer with the club after stepping down following the arrival of Mohammed Al Fayed to Craven Cottage.

But he will be delighted that the West London club are now heading back towards the big time.

The Key Man

Micky Adams

The former Southampton midfielder was in his first full season as player-manager and he could hardly have asked for a better start to his new career, could he? He led from the front as Fulham set the pace and, although he was bitterly disappointed to lose the title on goal difference, he still had plenty to smile about.

Stan Can Deliver

Look out the Premiership, here come Bury. At least they will be if they continue their tremendous rise.

Under the management of Stan Ternent, The Shakers have really shaken up the lower leagues in the past two seasons.

They won promotion from the Third Division in 1995-96, snatching third place by just one point, and followed that up by winning the Second Division Championship last term.

It's a tremendous achievement for one of football's unfashionable clubs, and is a reward for Ternent's organisational and motivational skills.

They lost just six League games last season - and none of them were at their Gigg Lane home - and that is top form by anyone's standards.

One thing's for sure, they won't be going into the First Division for the ride, and a few clubs will be in for a very dodgy ride from them.

The Key Man

Dean Kiely

One of the most highly-rated goalkeepers outside the Premiership and it was easy to see why last season. He was in stunning form as Bury conceded just 38 goals in their 46 League games last season. Incredibly, he conceded just seven in 23 home games and if he carries on like that next season Bury's biggest problem might be keeping him.

Football League Extra

Shooting

We salute the Nationwide heroes

The Premiership might be where all the money is, but they still know how to produce a good player in the lower divisions. Here are six of the best...

Georgi Kinkladze (Man City)
The little Georgian genius should be in the Premiership and if City fail to win promotion again this season then surely he will be.He is a player of undoubted class who has the ability to open up the tightest of defences, as he has proved on the international stage with his country. But that ability is matched by his loyalty and that has led to him signing a new contract at Maine Road. Georgians are fiercely proud people and 'Kinky' has not forgotten what City did for him when they first brought him over to England. But unless manager Frank Clark can build a team to match Kinkladze's ambition, then that loyalty could be stretched to breaking point.

Tony Thorpe (Luton)
He took the Second Division by storm last season, and surprised himself as much as anyone. Formerly an attacking midfielder, he was pushed up front early last term because of an injury crisis as Kenilworth Road, and never looked back.He scored 31 goals in his new role - including three hat-tricks - as Luton came within a whisker of an automatic promotion slot. Sadly, they just fell short of that mark and then suffered further disappointment when they were beaten in the play-offs by Crewe.But Thorpe, who was released as a youngster by Leicester, gives The Hatters cause for optimism that better days are coming to Town.

Gareth Ainsworth (Lincoln)
A highly-rated winger who suddenly found his scoring boots last season. Ainsworth was never a prolific goalscorer at his former club Preston but he found the net over 20 times last season as Lincoln just failed to make the play-offs.He was a real fans' favourite at Preston but a bout of glandular fever knocked his career back and he had to move to Sincil Bank to get back on track. And he did that in spectacular style. A big future beckons.

Dean Richards (Wolves)
One of the most highly-rated defenders outside the Premiership, Richards has a glittering future.He's still only 23 but already possesses all of the attributes to take him to the very top. He would like to achieve that with Wolves but it may be that 6ft 2in Richards needs to quit the gold and blacks to fulfill his dreams. Manchester United are known admirers and there was talk of a £5m offer not so long ago. If he continues to impress the big time won't be long in coming.

Stars

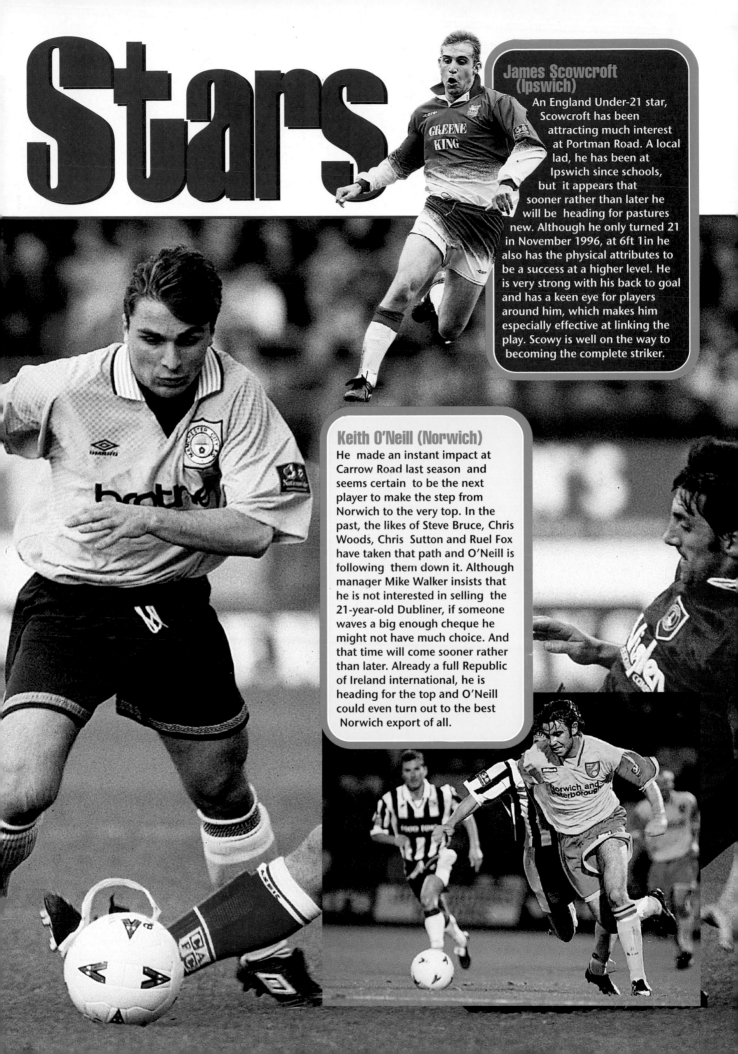

James Scowcroft (Ipswich)

An England Under-21 star, Scowcroft has been attracting much interest at Portman Road. A local lad, he has been at Ipswich since schools, but it appears that sooner rather than later he will be heading for pastures new. Although he only turned 21 in November 1996, at 6ft 1in he also has the physical attributes to be a success at a higher level. He is very strong with his back to goal and has a keen eye for players around him, which makes him especially effective at linking the play. Scowy is well on the way to becoming the complete striker.

Keith O'Neill (Norwich)

He made an instant impact at Carrow Road last season and seems certain to be the next player to make the step from Norwich to the very top. In the past, the likes of Steve Bruce, Chris Woods, Chris Sutton and Ruel Fox have taken that path and O'Neill is following them down it. Although manager Mike Walker insists that he is not interested in selling the 21-year-old Dubliner, if someone waves a big enough cheque he might not have much choice. And that time will come sooner rather than later. Already a full Republic of Ireland international, he is heading for the top and O'Neill could even turn out to the best Norwich export of all.

HOW THEY FINISHED

Who came where in the FA Carling Premiership and Scottish Leagues.

FA CARLING PREMIERSHIP

	P	W	D	L	F	A	Pts
Man Utd	38	21	12	5	76	44	75
Newcastle	38	19	11	8	73	40	68
Arsenal	38	19	11	8	62	32	68
Liverpool	38	19	11	8	62	37	68
Aston Villa	38	17	10	11	47	34	61
Chelsea	38	16	11	11	58	55	59
Sheff Wed	38	14	15	9	50	51	57
Wimbledon	38	15	11	12	49	46	56
Leicester	38	12	11	15	46	54	47
Tottenham	38	13	7	18	44	51	46
Leeds	38	11	13	14	28	38	46
Derby	38	11	13	14	45	58	46
Blackburn	38	9	15	14	42	43	42
West Ham	38	10	12	16	39	48	42
Everton	38	10	12	16	44	57	42
Southampton	38	10	11	17	50	56	41
Coventry	38	9	14	15	38	54	41
Sunderland	38	10	10	18	35	53	40
Middlesbrough*	38	10	12	16	51	60	39
Nott'm Forest	38	6	16	16	31	59	34

*Middlesbrough deducted three points

SCOTTISH PREMIER

	P	W	D	L	F	A	Pts
Rangers	36	25	5	6	85	33	80
Celtic	36	23	6	7	78	32	75
Dundee Utd	36	17	9	10	46	33	60
Hearts	36	14	10	12	46	43	52
Dunfermline	36	12	9	15	52	65	45
Aberdeen	36	10	14	12	45	54	44
Kilmarnock	36	11	6	19	41	61	39
Motherwell	36	9	11	16	44	55	38
Hibernian	36	9	11	16	38	55	38
Raith	36	6	7	23	29	73	25

SCOTTISH FIRST DIVISION

	P	W	D	L	F	A	Pts
St Johnstone	36	24	8	4	74	23	80
Airdrie	36	15	15	6	56	34	60
Dundee	36	15	13	8	47	33	58
St Mirren	36	17	7	12	48	41	58
Falkirk	36	15	9	12	42	39	54
Partick	36	12	12	12	49	48	48
Stirling	36	12	10	14	54	61	46
G'k Morton	36	12	9	15	42	41	45
Clydebank	36	7	7	22	31	59	28
East Fife	36	2	8	26	28	92	14

SCOTTISH SECOND DIVISION

	P	W	D	L	F	A	Pts
Ayr	36	23	8	5	61	33	77
Hamilton	36	22	8	6	75	28	74
Livingston	36	18	10	8	56	38	64
Clyde	36	14	10	12	42	39	52
Queen of South	36	13	8	15	55	57	47
Stenhousemuir	36	11	11	14	49	43	44
Brechin	36	10	11	15	36	49	41
Stranraer	36	9	9	18	29	51	36
Dumbarton	36	9	8	19	44	66	35
Berwick	36	4	11	21	32	75	23

SCOTTISH THIRD DIVISION

	P	W	D	L	F	A	Pts
Inverness CT	36	23	7	6	70	37	76
Forfar	36	19	10	7	74	45	67
Ross County	36	20	7	9	58	41	67
Alloa	36	16	7	13	50	47	55
Albion	36	13	10	13	50	47	49
Montrose	36	12	7	17	46	62	43
Cowdenbeath	36	10	9	17	38	51	39
Queen's Park	36	9	9	18	46	59	36
East Stirling	36	8	9	19	36	58	33
Arbroath	36	6	13	17	31	52	31

Who came where in the Nationwide League and Vauxhall Conference

FIRST DIVISION

	P	W	D	L	F	A	PTS
Bolton	46	28	14	4	100	53	98
Barnsley	46	22	14	10	76	55	80
Wolves	46	22	10	14	68	51	76
Ipswich	46	20	14	12	68	50	74
Sheff Utd	46	20	13	13	75	52	73
C.Palace	46	19	14	13	78	48	71
Portsmouth	46	20	8	18	59	53	68
Port Vale	46	17	16	13	58	55	67
QPR	46	18	12	16	64	60	66
Birmingham	46	17	15	14	52	48	66
Tranmere	46	17	14	15	63	56	65
Stoke	46	18	10	18	51	57	64
Norwich	46	17	12	17	63	68	63
Man City	46	17	10	19	59	60	61
Charlton	46	16	11	19	52	66	59
West Brom	46	14	15	17	68	72	57
Oxford	46	16	9	21	64	68	57
Reading	46	15	12	19	58	67	57
Swindon	46	15	9	22	52	71	54
Huddersfield	46	13	15	18	48	61	54
Bradford	46	12	12	22	47	72	48
Grimsby	46	11	13	22	60	81	46
Oldham	46	10	13	23	51	66	43
Southend	46	8	15	23	42	86	39

SECOND DIVISION

	P	W	D	L	F	A	PTS
Bury	46	24	12	10	62	38	84
Stockport	46	23	13	10	59	41	82
Luton	46	21	15	10	71	45	78
Brentford	46	20	14	12	56	43	74
Bristol C	46	21	10	15	69	51	73
Crewe	46	22	7	17	56	47	73
Blackpool	46	18	15	13	60	47	69
Wrexham	46	17	18	11	54	50	69
Burnley	46	19	11	16	71	55	68
Chesterfield	46	18	14	14	42	39	68
Gillingham	46	19	10	17	60	59	67
Walsall	46	19	10	17	54	53	67
Watford	46	16	19	11	45	38	67
Millwall	46	16	13	17	50	55	61
Preston	46	18	7	21	49	55	61
Bournemouth	46	15	15	16	43	45	60
Bristol R	46	15	11	20	47	50	56
Wycombe	46	15	10	21	51	56	55
Plymouth	46	12	18	16	47	58	54
York	46	13	13	20	47	68	52
Peterborough	46	11	14	21	55	73	47
Shrewsbury	46	11	13	22	49	74	46
Rotherham	46	7	14	25	39	70	35
Notts County	46	7	14	25	33	59	35

THIRD DIVISION

	P	W	D	L	F	A	PTS
Wigan	46	26	9	11	84	51	87
Fulham	46	25	12	9	72	38	87
Carlisle	46	24	12	10	67	44	84
Northampton	46	20	12	14	67	44	72
Swansea	46	21	8	17	62	58	71
Chester	46	18	16	12	55	43	70
Cardiff	46	20	9	17	56	54	69
Colchester	46	17	17	12	62	51	68
Lincoln	46	18	12	16	70	69	66
Cambridge	46	18	11	17	53	59	65
Mansfield	46	16	16	14	47	45	64
Scarborough	46	16	15	15	65	68	63
Scunthorpe	46	18	9	19	59	62	63
Rochdale	46	14	16	16	58	58	58
Barnet	46	14	16	16	46	51	58
L.Orient	46	15	12	19	49	58	57
Hull	46	13	18	15	44	49	57
Darlington	46	14	10	22	64	78	52
Doncaster	46	14	10	22	52	66	52
Hartlepool	46	14	9	23	53	66	51
Torquay	46	13	11	22	46	62	50
Exeter	46	12	12	22	48	73	48
Brighton*	46	13	10	23	53	70	47
Hereford	46	11	14	21	50	65	47

*Brighton deducted two points

VAUXHALL CONFERENCE

	P	W	D	L	F	A	PTS
Macclesfield	42	27	9	6	80	30	90
Kidderminster	42	26	7	9	84	42	85
Stevenage	42	24	10	8	87	53	82
Morecambe	42	19	9	14	69	56	66
Woking	42	18	10	14	71	63	64
Northwich	42	17	12	13	61	54	63
Farnborough	42	16	13	13	58	53	61
Hednesford	42	16	12	14	52	50	60
Telford	42	16	10	16	46	56	58
Gateshead	42	15	11	16	59	63	56
Southport	42	15	10	17	51	61	55
Rushden & D	42	14	11	17	61	63	53
Stalybridge	42	14	10	18	53	58	52
Kettering	42	14	9	19	53	62	51
Hayes	42	12	14	16	54	55	50
Slough	42	12	14	16	62	65	50
Dover	42	12	14	16	57	68	50
Welling	42	13	9	20	50	60	48
Halifax	42	12	12	18	55	74	48
Bath	42	12	11	19	53	80	47
Bromsgrove	42	12	5	25	41	67	41
Altrincham	42	9	12	21	49	73	39

DES WALKER
SHEFF. WEDNESDAY
SHOOT

Meet the bosses staging an...

Internat rescue

These are the men with their heads on the block! Success can mean immortality, failure a spectre that can haunt them for ever. Managing your country is not a job for the faint-hearted. These are the men for whom the risks are high - the bosses of the home nations.

ENGLAND - GLENN HODDLE

Appointed:	June 1996.
Born:	27th November 1957 in Hayes.
Playing career:	Tottenham - Monaco - Swindon - Chelsea.
Honours:	England . . . . .53 caps, 8 goals.
	Tottenham . . . . . .FA Cup winner (twice)
	UEFA Cup winner
	Monaco . . . . .French Championship
Management clubs:	Swindon - Chelsea
Honours:	Swindon . . . . . . .Promotion to Premier 1993.
	Chelsea . . . . .FA Cup runners-up 1994.

Fame claim:
World class as a player with great skill and vision. Popular choice to follow Terry Venables.

Previous Managers:

Walter Winterbottom	1946 - 1962
Alf Ramsey	1963 - 1974
Joe Mercer (caretaker)	1974
Don Revie	1974 - 1977
Ron Greenwood	1977 - 1982
Bobby Robson	1982 - 1990
Graham Taylor	1990 - 1993
Terry Venables	1993 - 1996

SCOTLAND
CRAIG BROWN

Appointed:	November 1993.
Born:	1st July 1951 in Miravene.
Playing career:	Rangers - Dundee - Falkirk.
Honours:	Scotland caps at junior, schoolboy and youth levels.
	Dundee . . . . . Scottish Championship.
Management career:	Assistant manager at Motherwell Manager at Clyde Assistant manager of Scotland.
Honours:	Clyde . . . . Scottish Second Division Championship.

Fameclaim:
Playing career wrecked by injury. Became a schoolteacher and headmaster until Ian St John took him to Motherwell as his second-in-command.

Previous Managers:

Bobby Brown	1967 - 1971
Tommy Docherty	1971 - 1972
Willie Ormond	1973 - 1977
Ally Macleod	1977 - 1978
Jock Stein	1978 - 1985
Alex Ferguson (caretaker)	1985 - 1986
Andy Roxburgh	1986 - 1993

REP OF IRE
MICK
McCARTHY

Appointed:	February 1996.
Born:	7th February 1959 in Barnsley.
Playing career:	Barnsley - Manchester City - Celtic - Lyon - Millwall
Honours:	Republic of Ireland . . 57 caps, 2 goals.
	Celtic - . . . . Scottish Championship. Scottish FA Cup (twice)
Management career:	Millwall.

Fame claim:
Captained the Republic in the 1990 World Cup and led them to an historic victory over Italy. People's choice to replace Jack Charlton.

Previous Managers:

Liam Tuohy	1971 - 1972
Johnny Giles	1973 - 1980
Eoin Hand	1980 - 1985
Jack Charlton	1986 - 1995

WALES
BOBBY GOULD

Appointed:	August 1995
Born:	12th June 1948 in Coventry
Playing career:	Coventry-Arsenal-Wolves (twice)-Bristol City-West Brom-West Ham-Bristol Rovers-Hereford-Wimbledon-Aldershot.
Honours:	Coventry . . . . Division Two Championship Wolves. . . . . Division Two Championship West Ham . . . . FA Cup winners
Management career:	Bristol Rovers - Coventry (twice) - Bristol City - Wimbledon West Brom.
Honours:	Wimbledon . . . . FA Cup winners.

Fame claim:
An exciting forward with a long playing career. He then took his skills into coaching and management, and was even a TV presenter with Sky before landing the Wales job.

Previous Managers:

Mike Smith	1974 - 1979
Mike England	1980 - 1988
David Williams (caretaker)	1988
Terry Yorath	1988 - 1993
John Toshack	1994
Mike Smith	1994 - 1995

N. IRELAND
BRYAN
HAMILTON

Appointed:	February 1994.
Born:	21st December 1946, in Belfast
Playing career:	Distillery-Linfield-Ipswich-Everton-Millwall-Swindon-Tranmere.
Honours:	Northern Ireland . . . . . 50 caps, 4 goals Everton . . . . League Cup Finalist
Management career:	Tranmere - Wigan - Leicester

Fame claim:
Much respected international who became the first full-time manager appointed by Northern Ireland. Popular choice because of his playing record for his country.

Previous Managers:

Billy Bingham	1967 - 1971
Terry Neill	1971 - 1975
Dave Clements	1975 - 1976
Danny Blanchflower	1976 - 1979
Billy Bingham	1980 - 1993

England's top guardsman

You could put him between the gate posts at Buckingham Palace or the Tower of London and nobody would get past him. That's how England fans view their favourite goalie, the penalty king and top guardsman - DAVID SEAMAN MBE.

SEAMAN ON ENGLAND

There's nothing quite like playing for England. I have had some great times with my clubs but it is completely different when you are playing for England. There have been several set-backs through injury and, since we always produce top goalkeepers in this country, it is easy to think that you will never get a chance - but it has come right for me. Playing for England gains you a lot of respect, even from the opposition fans. It is something to be proud of.

SEAMAN ON WORLD CUP GLORY

All being well I shall be there in France for the 1998 World Cup. We were all disappointed at going out of the Euro'96 semis on penalties and we have been keen to try and put the record straight ever since. I couldn't watch the Euro'96 final as it would have been torture knowing how close we came to being there. I don't plan to watch the 1998 World Cup final either - I want to be playing in it!

SEAMAN ON ARSENAL

It is a great club - one of the best in the world. We were close to being the finished article last season, and everyone was saying that if Arsene Wenger had been with us from the start we would have won the championship. We have a great chance this sea-

son to do just that and our confidence is really high. We want to do well in Europe as well and we believe that we can. There have been a lot of changes in training, and even diet, and the whole approach is different. I'm sure that there's going to be a celebration or two at Highbury come the end of this season!

SEAMAN ON GOALKEEPING

It's not so bad if you are busy. You see plenty of the ball and it keeps you on your toes. You don't want to be busy of course - you want the ball to be at the other end, but then, if your team is too much on top you start to worry. You stand there thinking that you're suddenly going to be called into making a finger-tip save when you've had nothing to do for ages.

SEAMAN FACTS

Full name: David Andrew Seaman.

Born: Rotherham, 19th September 1963.

Height: 6ft 4ins.

Weight: 14st 10lbs.

Clubs:
Leeds - apprentice to pro on 22nd September 1981.
Peterborough - 13th August 1982 - £4,000
Birmingham - 5th October 1984 - £100,000
Queens Park Rangers - 7th August 1986 - £225,000
Arsenal - 18th May 1990 - £1.3 million

Senior debut:
28th August 1982, for Peterborough v Stockport. Drew 1-1.

International Career:
England caps at Under-21 and senior levels.

Honours:
Arsenal - League Championship 1991.
FA Cup 1993
Coca-Cola Cup 1993
European Cup Winners' Cup 1994
MBE 1996

DAVID SEAMAN
ENGLAND
SHOOT

Gary Mac
the tartan terror

If you want to know the identity of Scotland's danger-man - ask any of their opponents! They know who they try to stifle. Go ahead - ask them! They'll all come up with the same answer - GARY McALLISTER!

McALLISTER ON SCOTLAND

For years Scotland has been looked upon as a 'nearly' team - but our day will come! We have a reputation for dogged determination, passion and pride but we have a lot of players with skill too. For me, there is nothing like playing for my country. Each occasion is very special and I hope to be able to go on playing at international level for a few years yet.

McALLISTER ON THE TARTAN ARMY

They are fantastic aren't they? Wherever they go they bring colour and fun to the game. In tournaments like the European Championship they steal the show and their presence is greatly appreciated by the players. When you see them there it is like having your star players turn up.

McALLISTER ON CAREER MOVES

I began with my local club, Motherwell, and won my first medal with them before joining Leicester. Probably my best move was when I joined Leeds in 1990, because it led to the League Championship, the European Cup and most of my Scotland caps. When I left to join Coventry, the time was right. All these moves have meant that I have played for some great managers.

McALLISTER ON PLAYING FOOTBALL

If you cut me open and had a look inside you would find soccer written all the way through. The game has given me a lot - a good wage, travel, adventure, great experiences, fun, fame, pride, and happiness. I intend playing at the top level at least until I am 35.

McALLISTER ON TIME OFF

You have to have some time off no matter what job you do. I suppose my chief relaxation is playing golf. I love the game and I was a Scottish schoolboy international. I also enjoy a good holiday in the summer. It is important to get away from the spotlight, unwind and recharge your batteries ready for the next season.

MAC FACTS

Full name: Gary McAllister.
Born: Motherwell, 25th December 1964.
Height: 6ft 1in.
Weight: 11st 5lbs.
Clubs:
Motherwell - signed in 1981.
Leicester - 15th August 1985 - £125,000.
Leeds - 2nd July 1990 - £1 million.
Coventry - 23rd July 1996 - £3 million.
Senior debut:
1st May 1981 for Motherwell v Queen of the South. Lost 2-5.
International career:
Scotland caps at Under-21, 'B' and senior levels.
Honours:

Motherwell -	Scottish Division One championship 1985.
Leeds -	League Championship 1992. Charity Shield 1992.

GARY McALLISTER
SCOTLAND
SHOOT

Roy of the Republic

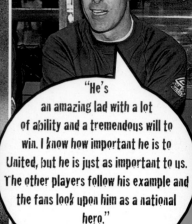

When you are a key player for Manchester United and Ireland, there might not seem much else to conquer - but don't say that to ROY KEANE - he's still hot on the trail of glory ... even though he is now a national hero in Ireland where they call him "Roy of the Republic"!

KEANE FACTS

Full name:	Roy Maurice Keane
Born:	Cork, 10th August 1971.
Height:	5ft 10ins.
Weight:	12st 10lbs.

Clubs:
Nottingham Forest - 12th June 1990 from Cobh Rangers - £10,000.
Manchester United - 22nd July 1993 - £3.75 million.

Senior debut:
28th August 1990 for Nottingham Forest v Liverpool. Lost 0-2.

International career:
Rep of Ireland caps - school, youth, Under-21 and senior levels.

Honours:
Nottingham Forest - ZDS Cup 1992.
Manchester United - Premiership Championship 1994, 1996, 1997. FA Cup 1994, 1996. Charity Shield 1993, 1996.

KEANE ON IRELAND

When we failed to beat Iceland in our home World Cup qualifier, and then slipped up away to Macedonia and Romania, we made life very difficult for ourselves. Playing in the 1994 World Cup in America was a fantastic experience but we were then disappointed not to reach Euro'96. There has been a lot of rebuilding since then and now we are ready to come again!

KEANE ON MANAGERS

When I started, Brian Clough was brilliant for me. He used to tell me off when I deserved it but he was a great motiva-tor and praised you when you did well. Alex Ferguson has the same type of approach, although he has his own style. He will give you a real dress-ing down if you have done wrong or not played well - but he is always right. For Ireland, I had Jack Charlton, and now Mick McCarthy, as managers - both top men. All four managers have added something to my game and made me a better player.

KEANE ON MANCHESTER UNITED

Being successful and winning trophies is every player's dream. Once you become a professional footballer you want to be among the best - and that is what it means to play for Manchester United, being among the very best! Old Trafford is a fantastic sta-dium, the supporters are bril-liant and the players are top class. That's what Manchester United is all about - class!

KEANE ON FORM

I had a few ups and downs last season because I had to have a knee operation just after the season started. Then, when I came back, I was out for a few more games with a dead leg. I had a suspension after that and then suffered another injury when playing against Rapid Vienna. It's a bit of a strain having to keep coming back like that but I have managed it each time and seem to have been play-ing all right - otherwise the gaffer would soon let me know that he wasn't happy!

KEANE ON GROWING-UP

I have matured a lot since I moved to Old Trafford. I think a lot more about my game and that reflects in my play. I am still an aggressive player , but I have learned to control it and I think that has made me a better player.

ROY KEANE
EIRE
SHOOT

The Speed
king of Wales

The World Cup has passed them by for another four years, but Wales still gave their fans a few good results to cheer. The Welsh might not win much silverware but they have a treasure trove of football talent, in which one of the jewels is the amazing GARY SPEED.

SPEED ON HIS CAREER

I could have chosen to become a cricketer as I played for Wales at schoolboy level. But I couldn't resist giving soccer a try and I have never regretted it. I was at Elland Road for ten years before I joined the team that I had supported as a boy - Everton. They were great days at Leeds and I had mixed feelings about leaving. I needed new challenges and Goodison was just the right place.

SPEED ON WALES

Since Terry Yorath left we have had several managers and it takes time for any internation-al manager to get things the way he wants. We have shown, in individual games, that we can match the best and when you look at players like Ryan Giggs, you can see that the talent is there. If we can only get some consistency there is no reason why we cannot qualify for a major tournament !

SPEED ON DREAMS

Some of my dreams have already come true. I have a career as a professional foot-baller and I have played for two of the biggest clubs in the country. I have won a few medals and played for my country, so I can't complain, can I? I still have lots of ambi-tion. I would like to play in the FA Cup final and win the Premiership and, of course, I would like to play for Wales in one or both of the two major tournaments. So I still have plenty to play for.

SPEED ON PROUD MOMENTS

Winning my first full cap for Wales was fantastic, but I have also taken a lot of pride in winning the League champi-onship and playing in Europe for Leeds - as well as pulling on an Everton shirt for the very first time.

SPEED ON TEAM-MATES

I have played alongside some of the best players in the game - stars like Gary McAllister, Gordon Strachan, Nick Barmby, Ryan Giggs, Eric Cantona, and many oth-ers. When you have team-mates like that you can't help but improve your own game. You have to get on well off the pitch too, because that's important for team spirit. I can't think of anyone that I haven't got on with. The craziest was David Batty - a good mate - but a lunatic!

SPEED FACTS

Full name: Gary Andrew Speed.
Born: Mancot, 8th September 1969.
Height: 5ft 11ins.
Weight: 12st 10lbs.
Clubs:
Leeds - trainee then full pro from 13th June 1988.
Everton - 1st June 1996 - £3.5 million.
Senior debut:
6th May 1989 for Leeds v Oldham. Drew 0-0.
International career:
Wales caps at youth, Under-21, and senior levels.
Honours:
Leeds - League Championship 1992.
Division Two championship 1990
Charity Shield 1992.

GARY SPEED
WALES
SHOOT

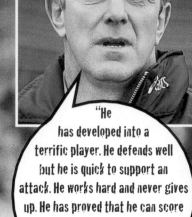

Lennon's
the Irish beat-all

There's a new mood sweeping through soccer in Northern Ireland. Suddenly, the Belfast boys are getting some good results again and the fans are singing. One of the main men behind the Irish revival is Leicester's NEIL LENNON - the new Ulster superstar.

LENNON ON LEICESTER

Life has been brilliant since I joined the Foxes in February 1996. A few months after I went to Leicester we beat Crystal Palace in the First Division play-off at Wembley. Then we had some great battles in the Premiership and ended the season with the Coca Cola Cup and a place in Europe. Who could ask for more?

LENNON ON HIS EARLIER CAREER

It was a disappointment to be given a free transfer by Manchester City in 1990, but my move to Crewe was great.

It is a terrific club, especially for young players - and playing for Dario Gradi certainly made a big difference to my career.

LENNON ON HIGHS AND LOWS

I was low when I was freed by Manchester City. But I have also enjoyed some great highs - joining Leicester and winning promotion to the Premiership, and then winning the Coca-Cola Cup. The proudest moment is probably walking out for the first time in a Northern Ireland senior shirt. My debut was in June 1994 in Miami. We lost 0-3 to Mexico, but it was still a great day for me.

LENNON ON THE FUTURE

At Leicester we want to improve on last season. We were very close to getting to the FA Cup final, and we would all like to make it to Wembley for that one.. For Northern Ireland, our sights are on the European Championship in 2000. If we can qualify for that it will be our first tournament finals since the 1986 World Cup. Having drawn away to Germany just after they won Euro'96, we believe that anything is possible for us.

LENNON ON NORTHERN IRELAND

We have come through a bit of a lean spell and things are

LENNON FACTS

Full name: Neil Paul Lennon.
Born: Lurgan, 25th June 1971.
Height: 5ft 10ins.
Weight: 12st 12lbs.
Clubs:
Manchester City - trainee then full pro from 26th August 1989.
Crewe - 9th August 1990 - free transfer.
Leicester City - 23rd February 1996 - £750,000.
Senior debut: 30th April 1988 for Manchester City v Birmingham. Won 3-0.
International career:
Northern Ireland caps at youth, Under-21, Under-23, 'B' and senior levels.
Honours:
Crewe - promotion from Division Three 1994.
Leicester - promotion from Division One 1996. Coca-Cola Cup 1997

getting much better now. There is good team spirit and we have much more confidence going into games. Bryan Hamilton is a good manager. Our performances have definitely improved and we are beginning to get results.

NEIL LENNON
N. IRELAND
SHOOT

Things can get a bit serious in the wonderful world of footie. But it's not all Mr Moody and Vinny Vicious. Plenty of players have a laugh on the pitch, not to mention us lot - the fans. SHOOT try to look on the lighter side of life every week and here, over the next few pages, are some of the high-laughs of last season....

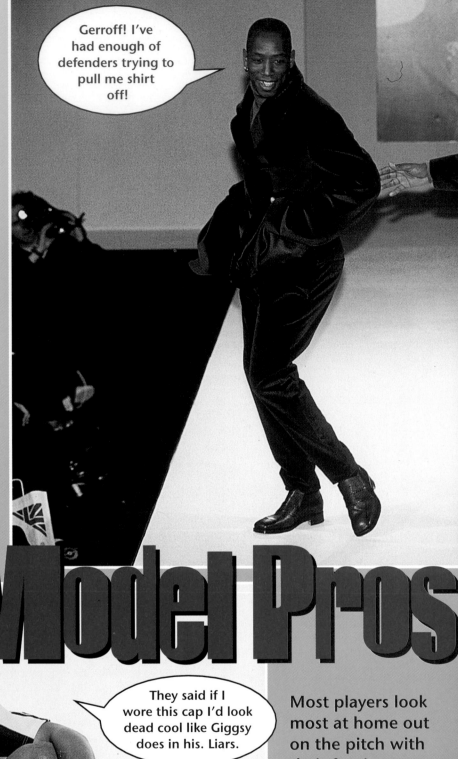

Gerroff! I've had enough of defenders trying to pull me shirt off!

Model Pros

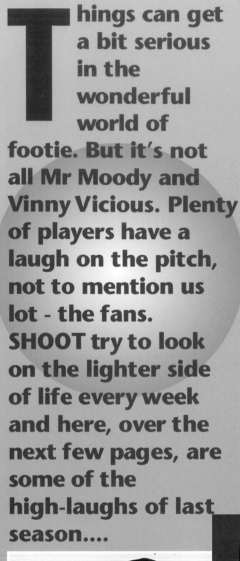

They said if I wore this cap I'd look dead cool like Giggsy does in his. Liars.

Most players look most at home out on the pitch with their footie gear on. But now and again, they get tempted into the wonderful world of fashion. The catwalks were not made for some of this lot but they put the blusher on and waltzed along regardless...

in the net

Sand storm

John Beck might have done a pretty good job at Lincoln last season but don't mention his name around Preston. His long ball style gave the players and fans there the hump. Beck was so determined to play his long ball tactics at Preston when he was boss there that he told the groundstaff to put sand in the corners of the plastic pitch to hold the ball up.

After a Premiership video viewing panel, six Premiership players have lost goals they scored last season. If you find any of them, please contact their clubs!

The missing goals are:-

Egil Ostenstad (Southampton) v Man United Oct 26

Jan-Aage Fjortoft (Middlesbro) v Liverpool Dec 14

WHERE'S ME GOAL?

Craig Russell (Sunderland) v Chelsea Dec 15

Savo Milosevic (A.Villa) v Wim'don Dec 22

Ashley Ward (Derby) v Chelsea Mar 1

Jamie Redknapp (Liverpool) v Everton Apr 16

So Sunderland's top scorer in 96-97 was **Paul Stewart** with a mighty four goals - sad - and **Jamie Redknapp** scored only one Premiership goal all season - double sad! Just like to say SHOOT always had Redders' effort in the derby as a Claus Thomsen og 'cos we're blinkin' clever!

AD ENOUGH!

Last year's World Cup clash between England and Poland turned into a sponsorship nightmare with several events scuppering the best laid plans of the marketing people...

● Match referee Meier decided the new England away kit would clash with the Poland strip and ordered Hod's boys to don the white home kit instead. It was to be the grand unveiling of the new red strip by Umbro but that had to be put on hold

● Umbro golden boy Alan Shearer was photographed celebrating the victory in a Poland shirt – with a Nike sign on the chest!

● During Channel 5's exclusive live coverage of the game, the advertising hoardings in the background were advertising Sky's exclusive coverage of Le Tournoi

Bit of a mare all round, really - 'part from the result that is!

GAGTASTIC

"**i've** got a false front tooth and when I was getting booked against Southampton I was telling the ref what I thought of him. That's when my tooth flew out and hit him in the face!" Who said that? Clue: he's ginger, he's a red and he's red, white and blue..

ANSWER OVERLEAF

WANNABEES

£15 MILL BECKS? YOU SURE?

We hear that the England squad were insured for £135m for their summer exploits in Manchester, Poland and France. But let's have a closer look at some of those valuations.

Any particular reason why Sol Campbell at £7 million should be worth £2m more than both the Neville brothers? And who would pay £5m for Gazza nowadays?

We presume the values are based on the players' sell-on fee plus potential earnings for the clubs they belong to.

So that's why Paul Scholes is a whopping £8m, Nicky Butt £7m and Andy Cole £7m, while Robert Lee's only £3m. Supposedly, the United kids will go on to win everything before them while Lee's at the peak of his career now.

But top of the pile come David Beckham at £15m and Alan Shearer at £20m. £15 mill for Becks?!?! Could Mr P Spice possibly be just a tinsy bit over-rated? Naa!

Mark Bright's career may be drawing to a close with a spell at Charlton, but other top strikers wish they were closer to Brighty. So close in fact, they want to be Mrs Mark Bright. And you know who that is, don't you? Yep, **Emile Heskey** wants to be...

MICHELLE GAYLE

STEP INTO...THE WONDERFUL WORLD OF ANDY GRAY'S MIND

Falkirk hero Andy Gray wants a big move to finish his career in style, but the former Spur might just be too bonkers to make it big...

In 1991, he played 45 minutes for England. Here was Graham Taylor's top tactical advice: "He told me to belt the ball out of play if I got it early on. It was a bit of a shock to hear the manager say that your first touch in an international was to kick the ball out of play."

But he forgave Taylor: "I love him to death. Things just didn't go right for him."

But he didn't like Marco

'And Jack Dee Thought He Loved Widgets' Gabbiadini: "I hated him. Palace sell Ian Wright for £2.5m to Arsenal and we buy this overweight guy from Sunderland. All he used to talk about was widget beer, widgets in cans."

But before the Scottish Cup Final last season, he finally went totally hatstand on us...

"It's like baking a cake or buying one. Do you chose Sainsbury's own or Mr Kipling? Obviously, you want Mr Kipling every time and we've got that Mr Kipling mixture at Falkirk."

Yeah, cheers, Andy.

in the net

Leg it, Howey

If you thought the pain of injury was the worse part about playing football, you should hear what Newcastle's Steve Howey went through to get better.

"I had the biggest needle I've ever seen stuck in my groin to pump dye into my stomach which was then flushed into my legs," said the 25-year-old defender.

"Another time I had six-inch needles stuck in the back of my legs and I had to run on the spot."

Hmm. Sounds lovely! But Howey's phobia of needles was helped by some of the best painkillers available.

"They had to give me an injection to face an injection," said the Toon Army's human pin cushion. "So sometimes I was drugged up to my eyeballs!"

BIONIC MAC

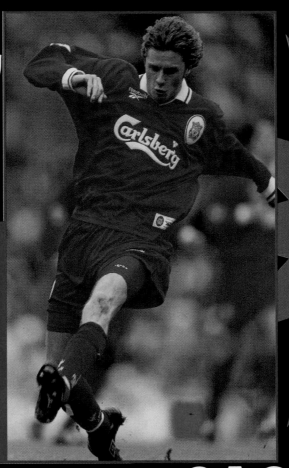

Everyone's having a say about their player of the year – now it's the turn of a computer. The statstastic Opta Index have voted Steve McManaman as their Player of the Year despite losing his form and needing an operation at the end of last season. Some other interesting facts include an astonishing 84% saves-to-goal ratio by Nigel Martyn, Middlesbrough winning 69% of their tackles and Wimbledon having the highest goals-to-shots ratio at 17%. And Karel Poborsky just beat Jamie Redknapp in the 'fiddling with his hair' competition with a last game of the season ruffle.

WHO ARE YA?

No wonder there's major fixture congestion thanks to billions of European games – Wales had FOUR teams in Europe this season! And that's from a League that doesn't even have their biggest clubs in it!

League of Wales champs Barry Town (who won the treble) were in the UEFA Cup, Cwmbran Town were in the Cup-Winners' Cup, League runners-up Inter Cable-Tel were also in the UEFA Cup.

But Ebbw Vale must have been well chuffed that they played in the Inter-Toto Cup while their rivals were sunbathing on a beach in Rhyl!

DOH!

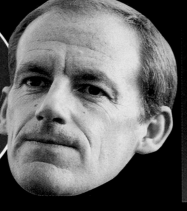

Asked what promotion to the Premiership would mean to him BEFORE the Play-Off Final, Palace boss Steve Coppell said: "Ten months of hell." You've had a 'mare, son!.

GAGTASTIC

ANSWER TO OUR HIGHLY HA-HA GAG-TELLER QUIZ...

The Gagmeister was none other than Man United and England cheeky monkey Nicky Butt. That tale comes from a new book called Football Funnies, a collection of crazy stories and best footie gags as told by top names from the footie world like Butt, Gary Neville, Chris Waddle and more. It's been made to raise money for Ware Youth FC. You can buy it for £5 (inc. p & p) from Tony Baker, 1 Hampden Hill, Ware, Herts SG12 7JT

Steady Eddie?

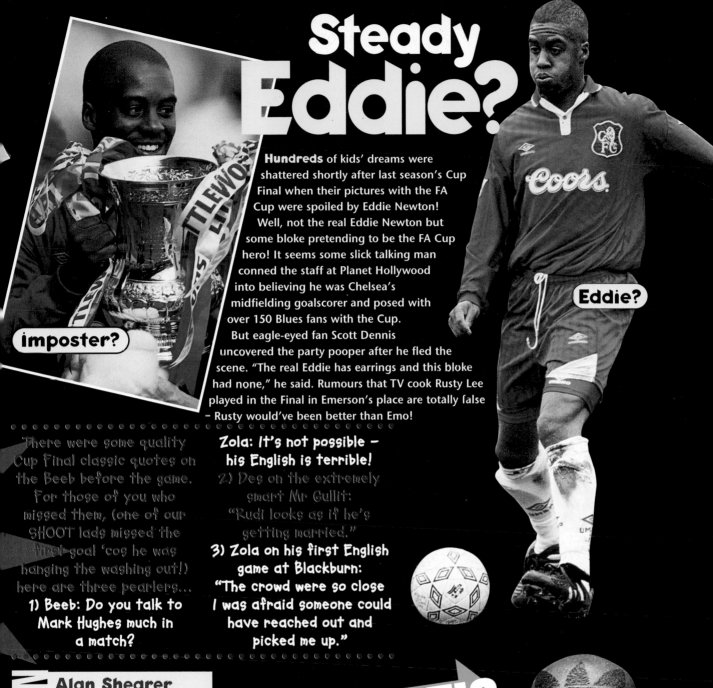

imposter?

Eddie?

Hundreds of kids' dreams were shattered shortly after last season's Cup Final when their pictures with the FA Cup were spoiled by Eddie Newton! Well, not the real Eddie Newton but some bloke pretending to be the FA Cup hero! It seems some slick talking man conned the staff at Planet Hollywood into believing he was Chelsea's midfielding goalscorer and posed with over 150 Blues fans with the Cup. But eagle-eyed fan Scott Dennis uncovered the party pooper after he fled the scene. "The real Eddie has earrings and this bloke had none," he said. Rumours that TV cook Rusty Lee played in the Final in Emerson's place are totally false – Rusty would've been better than Emo!

There were some quality Cup Final classic quotes on the Beeb before the game. For those of you who missed them, (one of our SHOOT lads missed the first goal 'cos he was hanging the washing out!) here are three pearlers...

1) Beeb: Do you talk to Mark Hughes much in a match?

Zola: It's not possible – his English is terrible!

2) Des on the extremely smart Mr Gullit: "Rudi looks as if he's getting married."

3) Zola on his first English game at Blackburn: **"The crowd were so close I was afraid someone could have reached out and picked me up."**

SHEAR DETERMINATION

Alan Shearer admitted he nearly lost his rag in the bruising World Cup encounter with Poland.

England's goalscoring hero was kicked all over the field during the 2-0 win but kept his cool to set up that titanic clash with Italy to see who qualified for France 98.

"I found it very difficult to keep my temper," said Shearer. "At times I felt like taking a swing back at them but I knew if I did I'd let my country down."

HAIR-TASTIC

Crystal Palace's Bruce Dyer not only put in a blistering performance at Wembley against Sheffield United but he also turned heads with an eye-catching hairstyle. Having a symbol of a famous sports company shaved into his bonce, Bruce also has the word adidas put on which apparently stands for "All day I dream about scoring".

Mental brings you the...

Crazy World of Football

MEXICAN 'keeper Jorge Campos, the No.1 with the multicolour jerseys, is a busy man – he once played two games in one day. He turned out for Mexico against the USA and then half an hour later he was in action for his American club Los Angeles Galaxy. What's more, he played the last 20 minutes of the second game as a striker.

WE know all about toilet rolls, but this is ridiculous. In Bulgaria last season's Cup Final between CSKA and Levski got a bit out of hand. The game ended in a mass brawl in the players' tunnel after fans threw a live snake at the referee!

WITH so much trouble going on around the world, it's not surprising that there's a club in Moldova called FC Agro!

ITALIAN side club Avellino finally signed Argentinian striker Leonardo Ricatti...after the player agreed to get his hair cut! "There's no room for long-haired people at Avellino," said club president Antonio Sibilia. Fans gathered outside the town's two barbers to catch a glimpse of the player getting his hair cut.

WHAT is it about the French? Jean-Pierre Cyprien, a French defender who plays for Swiss League-leaders Neuchatel Xamax, was banned for nine months after aiming a Cantona-style kung-fu kick at the manager of opposing team St Gallen at the end of a League match. Cyprien's high-flying challenge on the touchline caught St Gallen manager Roger Heli where it hurts most – in the groin!

IN ROMANIA the chairman of Jiul Petrosani, Miron Cozma, has been banned from football for two years. His offence? Headbutting Dinamo Bucharest's Danut Lupu as the players left the pitch at half-time during a League match.

IF you think English players look silly with advertising slogans on their shirts, spare a thought for Dutch side TOP Oss. They're sponsored by Chicken Tonight!

REFEREE Oscar Roberto De Godoi is unlikely to win any fair play awards in Brazil after he sent-off five players and dished out 11 yellow cards in the League match between Corinthians and Sao Paulo. After the match the ref had to take a breathaliser test because players complained he was drunk!

ATLETICO Madrid had to play their opening games of the Spanish season at the home of their great rivals Real Madrid after their own pitch was destroyed by a plague of worms!

REFEREE Luiz Vila Nova took the law into his own hands when he was sending off a player in League match in Brazil. The ref took exception to something the player said and floored him with a fierce right hook!

EVER since wildman striker Edmundo was christened 'The Animal' people have been taking things a bit too literally in Brazil. When Edmundo signed for Flamengo he was greeted at the airport by two elephants, a tiger and a chimpanzee dressed in a Flamengo shirt! Then fans took dogs dressed in Flamengo shirts and hats to his first game . . . someone even took a giant tortoise with the club colours painted on its shell.

HEARD the one about Spurs doing the League and Cup double last season? It's true . . . but it was Cape Town Spurs, in South Africa.

THIS is the most bizarre sending-off we've ever come across. In Ecuador they use golf carts to carry injured players off the pitch. Only during a match between Espoli and Barcelona the driver of the golf cart wasn't looking where he was going and ran over Espoli's Atualfo Valencia! The player was so mad that he got and punched the driver and got sent-off!

IN FINLAND they like to give their teams silly names like MyPa, ROPS and KUPS. Then there's FC Jazz, who won the League in 1993. But our favourites are in the Second Division . . . FC Santa Claus.

THE CANTONA effect is spreading. In South Africa, Rabili Blackpool's manager Walter Rautmann needed treatment for a kidney injury after he was a victim of a kung-fu kick . . . from one of his own players! Defender Ahmed Gora Ebrahim was not happy at being substituted after just 16 minutes of a game against Umtata Buucks. He stormed off the pitch, launched his own Cantona-style attack on the coach . . . and was then taken away in a police van.

IN PERU they never do things by halves. Last year referee Felipe Compinez was stoned to death by fans after awarding a last-minute penalty in a crunch match!

A REAL Betis fan in Spain still takes his dad, who died last year, to matches – in a used milk carton! The dying man's last wish was to have his ashes taken to each Betis home game. And the only container that club officials would allow in the stadium was a plastic milk carton.

SOUTH AFRICAN international defender Mark Fish is a big hit with fans, who take dead fish with South African flags stuffed in the gills to matches.

A YOUNG fan was killed and 20 others injured in Bangladesh . . . because it was raining! Players from Mohammedan and Brothers Union refused to play after a downpour had made the pitch unplayable, they claimed. Police had to fire teargas to restore order as angry fans went on the rampage.

ATLETIC Bucharest's junior team in Romania were forced to flee from the pitch two minutes from time in a game they were losing 16-0 after fans threatened to strip them naked if they conceded two more goals! The Romanian FA failed to see the funny side and fined the club £10,000.

YOU won't believe this, but one of Vietnam's top sides are called Ho-Chi-Min City Police! They were involved in a crucial League match with Dong Thap Province and whoever won looked set to clinch the title. Ho-Chi-Min City Police lost 3-1 but, get this, riot police had to be called when the losing side started attacking the referee!

RUSSIAN side Rotor Volgograd are claiming their title chances have been wiped out . . . by a drunken linesman! In a crucial League game against Chernomerets, which they needed to win to stay in touch with the title race, Rotor say they had a perfectly good goal by Gennady Yesipov ruled out by a linesman who "was not in a sober state".

FLAMENGO'S recent 4-1 defeat by Rio rivals Vasco da Gama has had people all over Brazil cracking jokes about the game (Flamengo are the Man United of Brazil). One newspaper even dedicated a whole page to the best gags. But one fan took things a bit too far. The Flamengo fan, who works as a porter in a Rio apartment block, took such exception to jibes from a Vasco fan working in a nearby block that he went round to sort him out, pulled out a gun . . . and shot him dead.

THEY'RE still mad for it Brazil. In a Rio derby between Vasco da Gama and Botofago, play had to be held for 25 minutes after a pitch invasion...by directors of the two clubs! Botofago president said: "I told the referee he was a coward and a failure."

STEP aside Des Lynam, Diego Maradona is planning a career as a TV presenter! The Argentinian star, who has admitted he is finished as a player, wants his own TV show in Argentina and says he will be an ace interviewer.

A CLUB in Brazil has found a clever way to pay their players' wages. Money is so tight that club president Marcelo Calderelli, a cattle rancher, is paying the players in cows! Each player gets one cow for every point won. The word is there's a lot at steak this season!

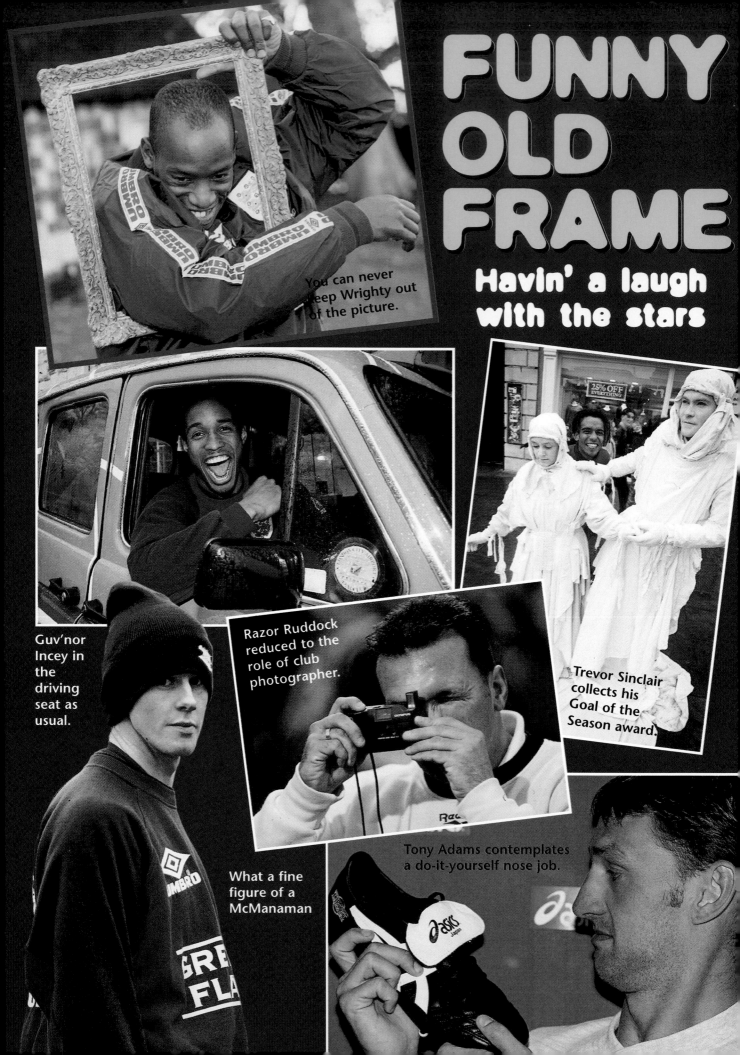

FUNNY OLD FRAME

Havin' a laugh with the stars

You can never keep Wrighty out of the picture.

Guv'nor Incey in the driving seat as usual.

Razor Ruddock reduced to the role of club photographer.

Trevor Sinclair collects his Goal of the Season award.

What a fine figure of a McManaman

Tony Adams contemplates a do-it-yourself nose job.

PIX of the YEAR

The pics in SHOOT are the best in the footie biz and our snappers never fail to get that magic moment on film. Last season was no different and here are six of the best from the cameras of SHOOT's top photographers - they were there when it really mattered...

BAR BLOW: Most Chesterfield fans would have been delighted to be 2-1 up against ten-man Middlesbrough in the FA Cup Semi-Final, but when Jonathan Howard's drive came back off the bar, they were livid it wasn't 3-1. The cameras showed it bounced well over the line but the ref waved play on and Boro clawed back into a 3-2 lead. The Second Division giant-killers did get a last minute equaliser but lost the replay. If only...

PIX of the YEAR

SIT DOWN NEXT TO ME: It's a bum job but someone's got to do it...and these Chelsea boys loved it! 1996-97 was a fab season for Ruud Gullit's lads and the arrival of France's Franck Leboeuf, and Italian duo Roberto di Matteo and Gianfranco Zola was an inspiration to the Brits in The Blues squad. But one famous face missing from most of the celebrations as Chelsea marched towards the FA Cup was Gianluca Vialli - he had to watch the fun from the touchline nearly all year.

PIX of the YEAR

NO GO GIGGSY: Liverpool's Jason McAteer and Michael Thomas make a red sandwich out of Ryan Giggs but the Man United star pulled through to race clear of Liverpool in the title race. The scousers' challenge flopped badly in the final few weeks despite coming close to victory at Old Trafford and other thrilling early season performances. But once Robbie Fowler got sent-off against Everton, the writing was on the wall – United's Title Again.

PIX of the YEAR

PRINCE PEARCE: We've seen this sort of joy from Stuart Pearce before - remember that penalty shoot-out against Spain in Euro 96? But while Pearce led Nottingham Forest to a string of surprise wins as soon as he took over as caretaker manager in early 1997, yells of delight were rare as they soon dropped back onto the bottom of the Premiership. One good point for Pearce was his continued place in the England squad at 35 - but life in Division One was not exactly what he had planned for this season.

PIX of the YEAR

LEAPFROG LOONIES: Tim Flowers and Ray Parlour get carried away with their air gymnastics. Blackburn were relegation certainties at Christmas while Arsenal were struggling to come to terms with Arsene Wenger's new tactics. But by the end of the season, mid-table Rovers were welcoming new boss Roy Hodgson and Arsenal were gutted at missing out on a Champions League place.

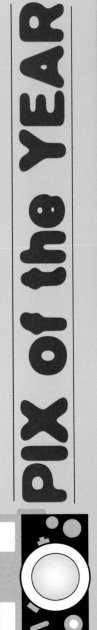

PIX of the YEAR

Facts-a-lot

All the stats from the 1996-97 season. Check out your club.

ARSENAL

Top League scorer:	Ian Wright (23)
League goals scored:	62
League goals conceded:	32
Highest attendance:	38,264 v Tottenham
Lowest attendance:	33,461 v Sheff Wed
Average attendance:	37,821
Total sendings-off:	5
Total bookings:	82

ASTON VILLA

Top League scorer:	Dwight Yorke (17)
League goals scored:	47
League goals conceded:	34
Highest attendance:	39,339 v Man Utd
Lowest attendance:	26,726 v Sheff Wed
Average attendance:	36,027
Total sendings-off:	2
Total bookings:	53

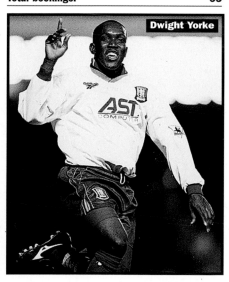
Dwight Yorke

BLACKBURN

Top League scorer:	Chris Sutton (11)
League goals scored:	42
League goals conceded:	43
Highest attendance:	30,476 v Man Utd
Lowest attendance:	19,214 v Derby
Average attendance:	24,966
Total sendings-off:	1
Total bookings:	61

Gianluca Vialli

CHELSEA

Top League scorer:	Gianluca Vialli (9)
League goals scored:	58
League goals conceded:	55
Highest attendance:	28,418 v Everton
Lowest attendance:	24,027 v Sunderland
Average attendance:	27,616
Total sendings-off:	2
Total bookings:	70

COVENTRY

Top League scorer:	Dion Dublin (14)
League goals scored:	38
League goals conceded:	54
Highest attendance:	23,085 v Man Utd
Lowest attendance:	15,273 v Wimbledon
Average attendance:	19,608
Total sendings-off:	5
Total bookings:	49

DERBY

Top League scorer:	Dean Sturridge (11)
League goals scored:	45
League goals conceded:	58
Highest attendance:	18,287 v Arsenal
Lowest attendance:	17,022 v Wimbledon
Average attendance:	17,888
Total sendings-off:	2
Total bookings:	62

EVERTON

Top League scorer:	Duncan Ferguson (10)
League goals scored:	44
League goals conceded:	57
Highest attendance:	40,177 v Liverpool
Lowest attendance:	30,368 v Leicester
Average attendance:	36,188
Total sendings-off:	2
Total bookings:	60

LEEDS

Top League scorers:	Brian Deane (5)
	Lee Sharpe (5)
League goals scored:	28
League goals conceded:	38
Highest attendance:	39,981 v Liverpool
Lowest attendance:	25,860 v Wimbledon
Average attendance:	32,117
Total sendings-off:	1
Total bookings:	79

LEICESTER

Top League scorer:	Steve Claridge (12)
League goals scored:	46
League goals conceded:	54
Highest attendance:	21,134 v Newcastle
Lowest attendance:	17,562 v Southampton
Average attendance:	20,183
Total sendings-off:	1
Total bookings:	51

Steve Claridge

LIVERPOOL

Top League scorer:	Robbie Fowler (18)
League goals scored:	62
League goals conceded:	37
Highest attendance:	40,892 v Man Utd
Lowest attendance:	36,126 v Nottm For
Average attendance:	39,776
Total sendings-off:	1
Total bookings:	44

MAN UTD

Top League scorer:	Ole Gunnar Solskjaer (18)
League goals scored:	76
League goals conceded:	44
Highest attendance:	55,314 v Wimbledon
Lowest attendance:	54,178 v Blackburn
Average attendance:	55,081
Total sendings-off:	1
Total bookings:	57

MIDDLESBROUGH

Top League scorer:	Fabrizio Ravanelli (16)
League goals scored:	51
League goals conceded:	60
Highest attendance:	30,215 v Tottenham
Lowest attendance:	29,485 v Sheff Wed
Average attendance:	29,870
Total sendings-off:	3
Total bookings:	73

NEWCASTLE

Top League scorer:	Alan Shearer (25)
League goals scored:	73
League goals conceded:	40
Highest attendance:	36,582 v Sunderland
Lowest attendance:	36,143 v Everton
Average attendance:	36,466
Total sendings-off:	2
Total bookings:	55

Alan Shearer

NOTTM FOR

Top League scorers:	Kevin Campbell (6)
	Alfe Inge Haaland (6)
League goals scored:	31
League goals conceded:	59
Highest attendance:	29,181 v Liverpool
Lowest attendance:	17,525 v Blackburn
Average attendance:	24,586
Total sendings-off:	0
Total bookings:	65

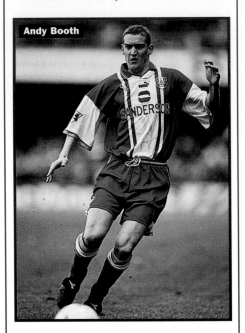

Andy Booth

SHEFF WED

Top League scorer:	Andy Booth (10)
League goals scored:	50
League goals conceded:	51
Highest attendance:	38,943 v Liverpool
Lowest attendance:	16,390 v Nottm For
Average attendance:	25,713
Total sendings-off:	3
Total bookings:	47

SOUTHAMPTON

Top League scorer:	Matt Le Tissier (13)
League goals scored:	50
League goals conceded:	56
Highest attendance:	15,253 v Man Utd
Lowest attendance:	14,418 v Wimbledon
Average attendance:	15,104
Total sendings-off:	4
Total bookings:	60

SUNDERLAND

Top League scorer:	Paul Stewart (4)
League goals scored:	35
League goals conceded:	53
Highest attendance:	22,512 v Derby
Lowest attendance:	18,642 v West Ham
Average attendance:	20,973
Total sendings-off:	5
Total bookings:	50

TOTTENHAM

Top League scorer:	Teddy Sheringham (7)
League goals scored:	44
League goals conceded:	51
Highest attendance:	33,040 v Leeds
Lowest attendance:	22,943 v Blackburn
Average attendance:	31,067
Total sendings-off:	1
Total bookings:	63

WEST HAM

Top League scorer:	Paul Kitson (8)
League goals scored:	39
League goals conceded:	48
Highest attendance:	25,064 v Liverpool
Lowest attendance:	19,105 v Aston Villa
Average attendance:	23,208
Total sendings-off:	2
Total bookings:	67

Paul Kitson

WIMBLEDON

Top League scorer:	Efan Ekoku (11)
League goals scored:	49
League goals conceded:	46
Highest attendance:	25,786 v Man Utd
Lowest attendance:	7,979 v Leeds
Average attendance:	15,138
Total sendings-off:	1
Total bookings:	38

First Division

BARNSLEY

Top League scorer:	Neil Redfearn (17)
League goals scored:	76
League goals conceded:	55
Highest attendance:	18,605 v Bradford
Lowest attendance:	6,337 v Oxford
Average attendance:	11,407
Total sendings-off:	1
Total bookings:	41

BIRMINGHAM

Top League scorer:	Paul Devlin (16)
League goals scored:	52
League goals conceded:	48
Highest attendance:	25,157 v Bradford
Lowest attendance:	13,033 v Bolton
Average attendance:	17,558
Total sendings-off:	5
Total bookings:	59

BOLTON

Top League scorer:	John McGinlay (24)
League goals scored:	100
League goals conceded:	53
Highest attendance:	22,024 v Charlton
Lowest attendance:	12,448 v Grimsby
Average attendance:	15,825
Total sendings-off:	4
Total bookings:	72

BRADFORD

Top League scorer:	Ole Sundgot (6)
League goals scored:	47
League goals conceded:	72
Highest attendance:	17,609 v Man City
Lowest attendance:	9,249 v Swindon
Average attendance:	12,925
Total sendings-off:	5
Total bookings:	53

Bruce Dyer

C.PALACE

Top League scorer:	Bruce Dyer (17)
League goals scored:	78
League goals conceded:	48
Highest attendance:	20,655 v Wolves
Lowest attendance:	11,382 v Stoke
Average attendance:	15,336
Total sendings-off:	4
Total bookings:	61

CHARLTON

Top League scorer:	Carl Leaburn (8)
League goals scored:	52
League goals conceded:	66
Highest attendance:	15,000 v C.Palace
Lowest attendance:	8,497 v Southend
Average attendance:	11,104
Total sendings-off:	5
Total bookings:	61

GRIMSBY

Top League scorer:	Clive Mendonca (18)
League goals scored:	60
League goals conceded:	81
Highest attendance:	8,732 v Man City
Lowest attendance:	3,532 v Oldham
Average attendance:	5,640
Total sendings-off:	3
Total bookings:	53

HUDDERSFIELD

Top League scorer:	Andy Payton (17)
League goals scored:	48
League goals conceded:	61
Highest attendance:	18,358 v Man City
Lowest attendance:	9,578 v Southend
Average attendance:	12,175
Total sendings-off:	6
Total bookings:	57

IPSWICH

Top League scorer:	Paul Mason (12)
League goals scored:	68
League goals conceded:	50
Highest attendance:	22,397 v Norwich
Lowest attendance:	7,086 v Swindon
Average attendance:	12,024
Total sendings-off:	1
Total bookings:	57

Paul Mason

MAN CITY

Top League scorer:	Uwe Rosler (15)
League goals scored:	59
League goals conceded:	60
Highest attendance:	30,729 v Oldham
Lowest attendance:	23,079 v Oxford
Average attendance:	26,753
Total sendings-off:	3
Total bookings:	56

NORWICH

Top League scorer:	Darren Eadie (17)
League goals scored:	63
League goals conceded:	68
Highest attendance:	20,256 v Ipswich
Lowest attendance:	11,946 v Portsmouth
Average attendance:	14,719
Total sendings-off:	7
Total bookings:	71

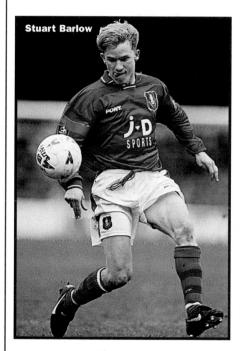

Stuart Barlow

OLDHAM

Top League scorer:	Stuart Barlow (12)
League goals scored:	51
League goals conceded:	66
Highest attendance:	12,992 v Man City
Lowest attendance:	4,851 v Oxford
Average attendance:	7,057
Total sendings-off:	1
Total bookings:	61

OXFORD

Top League scorer:	Nigel Jemson (18)
League goals scored:	64
League goals conceded:	68
Highest attendance:	9,223 v Reading
Lowest attendance:	6,334 v Bradford
Average attendance:	7,608
Total sendings-off:	3
Total bookings:	41

PORT VALE

Top League scorer:	Tony Naylor (17)
League goals scored:	58
League goals conceded:	55
Highest attendance:	14,396 v Stoke
Lowest attendance:	4,522 v C.Palace
Average attendance:	7,384
Total sendings-off:	0
Total bookings:	40

PORTSMOUTH

Top League scorer:	Lee Bradbury (15)
League goals scored:	59
League goals conceded:	53
Highest attendance:	12,841 v Man City
Lowest attendance:	5,579 v Southend
Average attendance:	8,853
Total sendings-off:	8
Total bookings:	62

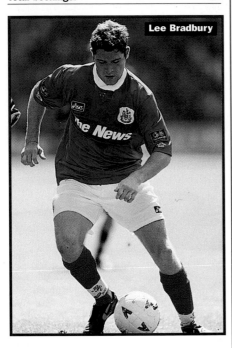

Lee Bradbury

QPR

Top League scorer:	John Spencer (17)
League goals scored:	64
League goals conceded:	60
Highest attendance:	17,376 v Wolves
Lowest attendance:	7,776 v Bradford
Average attendance:	12,553
Total sendings-off:	2
Total bookings:	54

READING

Top League scorer:	Trevor Morley (22)
League goals scored:	58
League goals conceded:	67
Highest attendance:	14,853 v Wolves
Lowest attendance:	5,513 v Tranmere
Average attendance:	9,164
Total sendings-off:	6
Total bookings:	67

Petr Katchouro

SHEFF UTD

Top League scorers:	Petr Katchouro (12)
	Andy Walker (12)
League goals scored:	75
League goals conceded:	52
Highest attendance:	25,596 v Stoke
Lowest attendance:	12,301 v Swindon
Average attendance:	16,644
Total sendings-off:	3
Total bookings:	63

SOUTHEND

Top League scorers:	Jeroen Boere (9)
	Andy Rammell (9)
League goals scored:	42
League goals conceded:	86
Highest attendance:	8,707 v Man City
Lowest attendance:	3,716 v Sheff Utd
Average attendance:	5,288
Total sendings-off:	3
Total bookings:	65

STOKE

Top League scorer:	Mike Sheron (18)
League goals scored:	51
League goals conceded:	57
Highest attendance:	22,500 v West Brom
Lowest attendance:	7,456 v Charlton
Average attendance:	12,747
Total sendings-off:	1
Total bookings:	41

SWINDON

Top League scorer:	Wayne Allison (11)
League goals scored:	52
League goals conceded:	71
Highest attendance:	14,374 v Man City
Lowest attendance:	6,730 v Southend
Average attendance:	9,264
Total sendings-off:	5
Total bookings:	62

TRANMERE

Top League scorer:	John Aldridge (18)
League goals scored:	63
League goals conceded:	56
Highest attendance:	14,309 v Bolton
Lowest attendance:	4,577 v Oxford
Average attendance:	8,170
Total sendings-off:	3
Total bookings:	63

WEST BROM

Top League scorer:	Andy Hunt (15)
	Paul Peschisolido (15)
League goals scored:	68
League goals conceded:	72
Highest attendance:	20,711 v Wolves
Lowest attendance:	11,792 v Southend
Average attendance:	15,131
Total sendings-off:	0
Total bookings:	49

Andy Hunt

WOLVES

Top League scorer:	Steve Bull (23)
League goals scored:	68
League goals conceded:	51
Highest attendance:	27,408 v Stoke
Lowest attendance:	21,072 v Charlton
Average attendance:	24,763
Total sendings-off:	2
Total bookings:	55

Second Division

BLACKPOOL

Top League scorer:	Tony Ellis (15)
League goals scored:	60
League goals conceded:	47
Highest attendance:	8,017 v Preston
Lowest attendance:	2,690 v Plymouth

Average attendance:	4,987
Total sendings-off:	8
Total bookings:	62

BOURNEMOUTH

Top League scorers:	Ian Cox (7)
	Steve Fletcher (7)
	Matt Holland (7)
	Steve Robinson (7)
League goals scored:	43
League goals conceded:	45
Highest attendance:	8,201 v Blackpool
Lowest attendance:	2,747 v Walsall
Average attendance:	4,603
Total sendings-off:	3
Total bookings:	45

BRENTFORD

Top League scorer:	Carl Asaba (23)
League goals scored:	56
League goals conceded:	43
Highest attendance:	8,679 v Watford
Lowest attendance:	3,675 v Notts Co
Average attendance:	5,824
Total sendings-off:	2
Total bookings:	42

Carl Asaba

BRISTOL CITY

Top League scorer:	Shaun Goater (23)
League goals scored:	69
League goals conceded:	51
Highest attendance:	18,674 v Bristol Rvs
Lowest attendance:	7,028 v Luton
Average attendance:	10,794
Total sendings-off:	4
Total bookings:	54

BRISTOL ROVERS

Top League scorer:	Peter Beadle (12)
League goals scored:	47
League goals conceded:	50

Highest attendance:	8,078 v Bristol City
Lowest attendance:	4,123 v Burnley
Average attendance:	5,629
Total sendings-off:	3
Total bookings:	47

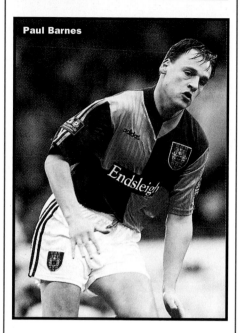

Paul Barnes

BURNLEY

Top League scorer:	Paul Barnes (24)
League goals scored:	71
League goals conceded:	55
Highest attendance:	16,186 v Preston
Lowest attendance:	7,875 v Rotherham
Average attendance:	10,041
Total sendings-off:	1
Total bookings:	51

BURY

Top League scorer:	Mark Carter (12)
League goals scored:	62
League goals conceded:	38
Highest attendance:	9,785 v Millwall
Lowest attendance:	2,690 v Shrewsbury
Average attendance:	4,500
Total sendings-off:	5
Total bookings:	57

CHESTERFIELD

Top League scorer:	Jon Howard (9)
League goals scored:	42
League goals conceded:	39
Highest attendance:	8,690 v Stockport
Lowest attendance:	2,805 v Peterborough
Average attendance:	4,638
Total sendings-off:	3
Total bookings:	33

CREWE

Top League scorer:	Dele Adebola (16)
League goals scored:	56
League goals conceded:	47

Highest attendance:	4,858 v Chesterfield
Lowest attendance:	3,125 v Notts Co
Average attendance:	3,978
Total sendings-off:	2
Total bookings:	27

GILLINGHAM

Top League scorer:	Iffy Onuora (21)
League goals scored:	60
League goals conceded:	59
Highest attendance:	9,305 v Millwall
Lowest attendance:	3,575 v Crewe
Average attendance:	6,032
Total sendings-off:	5
Total bookings:	88

LUTON

Top League scorer:	Tony Thorpe (28)
League goals scored:	71
League goals conceded:	45
Highest attendance:	9,347 v Stockport
Lowest attendance:	4,401 v York
Average attendance:	6,293
Total sendings-off:	4
Total bookings:	48

Steve Crawford

MILLWALL

Top League scorer:	Steve Crawford (11)
League goals scored:	50
League goals conceded:	55
Highest attendance:	9,371 v Wrexham
Lowest attendance:	5,202 v Notts Co
Average attendance:	7,729
Total sendings-off:	2
Total bookings:	72

NOTTS CO

Top League scorer:	Gary Martindale (6)
League goals scored:	33
League goals conceded:	59
Highest attendance:	6,879 v Preston
Lowest attendance:	2,423 v Plymouth
Average attendance:	4,257
Total sendings-off:	2
Total bookings:	61

Scott Houghton

PETERBOROUGH

Top League scorer:	Scott Houghton (8)
League goals scored:	55
League goals conceded:	73
Highest attendance:	9,499 v Luton
Lowest attendance:	2,975 v Wrexham
Average attendance:	5,297
Total sendings-off:	4
Total bookings:	69

PLYMOUTH

Top League scorer:	Mike Evans (10)
League goals scored:	47
League goals conceded:	58
Highest attendance:	9,645 v Bristol City
Lowest attendance:	4,237 v Chesterfield
Average attendance:	6,494
Total sendings-off:	4
Total bookings:	63

PRESTON

Top League scorer:	David Reeves (11)
League goals scored:	49
League goals conceded:	55
Highest attendance:	14,626 v Blackpool
Lowest attendance:	7,004 v Luton
Average attendance:	9,411
Total sendings-off:	2
Total bookings:	44

ROTHERHAM

Top League scorer:	Earl Judejean (6)
League goals scored:	39
League goals conceded:	70
Highest attendance:	4,562 v Burnley
Lowest attendance:	1,797 v Brentford
Average attendance:	2,843
Total sendings-off:	1
Total bookings:	50

SHREWSBURY

Top League scorer:	Ian Stevens (17)
League goals scored:	49
League goals conceded:	74
Highest attendance:	5,341 v Preston
Lowest attendance:	1,610 v Bournemouth
Average attendance:	3,178
Total sendings-off:	4
Total bookings:	53

STOCKPORT

Top League scorer:	Brett Angell (15)
League goals scored:	59
League goals conceded:	41
Highest attendance:	9,463 v Wycombe
Lowest attendance:	3,446 v Bournemouth
Average attendance:	6,423
Total sendings-off:	2
Total bookings:	47

Brett Angell

WALSALL

Top League scorer:	Kyle Lightbourne (20)
League goals scored:	54
League goals conceded:	53
Highest attendance:	6,306 v Burnley
Lowest attendance:	2,659 v Wycombe
Average attendance:	3,891
Total sendings-off:	5
Total bookings:	38

WATFORD

Top League scorer:	Tommy Mooney (13)
League goals scored:	45
League goals conceded:	38
Highest attendance:	14,109 v Luton
Lowest attendance:	6,139 v Bristol Rvs
Average attendance:	8,893
Total sendings-off:	3
Total bookings:	73

Karl Connolly

WREXHAM

Top League scorer:	Karl Connolly (14)
League goals scored:	54
League goals conceded:	50
Highest attendance:	6,947 v Burnley
Lowest attendance:	2,002 v Rotherham
Average attendance:	4,119
Total sendings-off:	4
Total bookings:	54

WYCOMBE

Top League scorers:	David Carroll (9)
	Steve McGavin (9)
League goals scored:	51
League goals conceded:	56
Highest attendance:	8,438 v Watford
Lowest attendance:	3,438 v Rotherham
Average attendance:	5,227
Total sendings-off:	6
Total bookings:	52

YORK

Top League scorers:	Nigel Pepper (12)
	Neil Tolson (12)
League goals scored:	47
League goals conceded:	68
Highest attendance:	5,958 v Burnley
Lowest attendance:	2,136 v Walsall
Average attendance:	3,358
Total sendings-off:	5
Total bookings:	38

BARNET

Top League scorer:	Sean Devine (11)
League goals scored:	46
League goals conceded:	51
Highest attendance:	3,316 v Fulham
Lowest attendance:	1,194 v Lincoln
Average attendance:	2,141
Total sendings-off:	6
Total bookings:	48

BRIGHTON

Top League scorer:	Craig Maskell (14)
League goals scored:	53
League goals conceded:	70
Highest attendance:	11,341 v Doncaster
Lowest attendance:	1,933 v Mansfield
Average attendance:	5,877
Total sendings-off:	4
Total bookings:	58

CAMBRIDGE

Top League scorers:	Micah Hyde (7)
	Mike Kyd (7)
	Scott McGleish (7)
League goals scored:	53
League goals conceded:	59
Highest attendance:	7,218 v Fulham
Lowest attendance:	2,033 v Scunthorpe
Average attendance:	3,380
Total sendings-off:	3
Total bookings:	60

CARDIFF

Top League scorer:	Steve White (13)
League goals scored:	56
League goals conceded:	54
Highest attendance:	6,144 v Fulham
Lowest attendance:	1,667 v Darlington
Average attendance:	3,563

Steve White

Total sendings-off:	4
Total bookings:	60

CARLISLE

Top League scorer:	Allan Smart (10)
League goals scored:	67
League goals conceded:	44
Highest attendance:	9,171 v Fulham
Lowest attendance:	3,839 v Cambridge
Average attendance:	5,401
Total sendings-off:	3
Total bookings:	53

Andy Milner

CHESTER

Top League scorer:	Andy Milner (12)
League goals scored:	55
League goals conceded:	43
Highest attendance:	4,005 v Wigan
Lowest attendance:	1,540 v Cardiff
Average attendance:	2,262
Total sendings-off:	6
Total bookings:	55

COLCHESTER

Top League scorer:	Tony Adcock (11)
League goals scored:	62
League goals conceded:	51
Highest attendance:	5,956 v Northampton
Lowest attendance:	1,842 v Scunthorpe
Average attendance:	3,254
Total sendings-off:	7
Total bookings:	50

DARLINGTON

Top League scorer:	Darren Roberts (16)
League goals scored:	64
League goals conceded:	78
Highest attendance:	4,662 v Hartlepool
Lowest attendance:	1,563 v Exeter
Average attendance:	2,791
Total sendings-off:	7
Total bookings:	57

DONCASTER

Top League scorer:	Colin Cramb (18)
League goals scored:	52
League goals conceded:	66
Highest attendance:	3,274 v Hull
Lowest attendance:	1,030 v Northampton
Average attendance:	2,087
Total sendings-off:	5
Total bookings:	65

EXETER

Top League scorer:	Darren Rowbotham (9)
League goals scored:	48
League goals conceded:	73
Highest attendance:	4,991 v Torquay
Lowest attendance:	2,155 v Carlisle
Average attendance:	3,014
Total sendings-off:	1
Total bookings:	56

FULHAM

Top League scorer:	Mike Conroy (21)
League goals scored:	72
League goals conceded:	38
Highest attendance:	11,479 v Northampton
Lowest attendance:	4,423 v Barnet
Average attendance:	6,642
Total sendings-off:	3
Total bookings:	75

Mike Conroy

HARTLEPOOL

Top League scorer:	Joe Allon (9)
League goals scored:	53
League goals conceded:	66
Highest attendance:	3,799 v Darlington
Lowest attendance:	1,120 v Cardiff
Average attendance:	2,085
Total sendings-off:	4
Total bookings:	79

Adrian Foster

HEREFORD

Top League scorer:	Adrian Foster (15)
League goals scored:	50
League goals conceded:	65
Highest attendance:	8,532 v Brighton
Lowest attendance:	1,363 v Lincoln
Average attendance:	2,942
Total sendings-off:	4
Total bookings:	56

HULL

Top League scorer:	Duane Darby (13)
League goals scored:	44
League goals conceded:	50
Highest attendance:	5,414 v Scunthorpe
Lowest attendance:	1,775 v Torquay
Average attendance:	3,412
Total sendings-off:	5
Total bookings:	65

L. ORIENT

Top League scorer:	Alex Inglethorpe (8)
League goals scored:	50
League goals conceded:	58
Highest attendance:	7,125 v Fulham
Lowest attendance:	2,406 v Rochdale
Average attendance:	4,273
Total sendings-off:	6
Total bookings:	61

LINCOLN

Top League scorer:	Alan Ainsworth (22)
League goals scored:	70
League goals conceded:	69
Highest attendance:	6,495 v Rochdale
Lowest attendance:	2,033 v Carlisle
Average attendance:	3,163
Total sendings-off:	3
Total bookings:	73

MANSFIELD

Top League scorer:	John Doolan (6)
League goals scored:	47
League goals conceded:	45
Highest attendance:	4,375 v Carlisle
Lowest attendance:	1,505 v Barnet
Average attendance:	2,282
Total sendings-off:	5
Total bookings:	61

NORTHAMPTON

Top League scorer:	Simon Grayson (12)
League goals scored:	67
League goals conceded:	44
Highest attendance:	6,828 v Scunthorpe
Lowest attendance:	3,519 v Hull
Average attendance:	4,822
Total sendings-off:	3
Total bookings:	63

Simon Grayson

ROCHDALE

Top League scorers:	Alex Russell (9)
	Steve Whitehall (9)
League goals scored:	58
League goals conceded:	58
Highest attendance:	3,320 v Carlisle
Lowest attendance:	1,074 v Hereford
Average attendance:	1,827
Total sendings-off:	4
Total bookings:	48

SCARBOROUGH

Top League scorer:	Gareth Williams (10)
League goals scored:	65
League goals conceded:	68
Highest attendance:	3,607 v Lincoln
Lowest attendance:	1,573 v Cambridge
Average attendance:	2,454
Total sendings-off:	3
Total bookings:	46

SCUNTHORPE

Top League scorer:	Phil Clarkson (13)
League goals scored:	59
League goals conceded:	62
Highest attendance:	4,257 v Hull
Lowest attendance:	1,524 v Chester
Average attendance:	2,605
Total sendings-off:	0
Total bookings:	48

David Penney

SWANSEA

Top League scorer:	David Penney (13)
League goals scored:	62
League goals conceded:	58
Highest attendance:	7,340 v Carlisle
Lowest attendance:	2,227 v Wigan
Average attendance:	3,817
Total sendings-off:	5
Total bookings:	68

TORQUAY

Top League scorer:	Rodney Jack (10)
League goals scored:	46
League goals conceded:	62
Highest attendance:	4,021 v Exeter
Lowest attendance:	1,087 v Rochdale
Average attendance:	2,288
Total sendings-off:	2
Total bookings:	53

WIGAN

Top League scorer:	Graeme Jones (31)
League goals scored:	84
League goals conceded:	51
Highest attendance:	7,106 v Mansfield
Lowest attendance:	2,606 v Doncaster
Average attendance:	3,898
Total sendings-off:	4
Total bookings:	58

LEE BOWYER
SHOOT
LEEDS

The Global

European football is now more popular and more accessible in this country than ever before. With so much footie from around the globe now shown on satellite **TV**, players such as Baggio, Del Piero and Ronaldo are now as much household names as the likes of Beckham, Fowler and Shearer. But while countries such as Spain, France and Germany continue to produce great players and great teams, one country stands apart from all the others. That country is Italy, and one team in particular stands apart from all the others, even in Serie A. That team is Juventus. SHOOT pays tribute to the best club side in the world...

Ju Beauties!

Juventus are one of the most famous teams in the world. At the moment, they are also arguably the best, despite losing their European crown to Borussia Dortmund. Over the last couple of years they have been European Champions, World Club Champions, Italian Champions...the list just goes on for Marcello Lippi's all-conquering side. Since winning the Champions' Cup in 1996, with more than a little help from Gianluca Vialli and Fabrizio Ravanelli, Juve

have gone from strength to strength, despite selling that formidable front pairing. Coach Lippi decided that he had had the best out of Messrs Vialli and Ravanelli so he packed them off to England. The fact that Juventus haven't missed them says everything about their squad. In fact, instead of struggling without that international strike-force, Juve have actually got even better. They totally dominated Serie A last season and it was no surprise when they wrapped up the title again. You can see why most people reckon Juve are in another league just at the moment. Indeed, Dutch ace Frank De Boer admitted pretty much that after his Ajax side had been destroyed 4-1 by Juve in the European Cup in Turin last April.
De Boer confessed:
"I can't remember when we last let in four goals in a European match. Juventus are like a team from another planet."

Stars in Stripes

These are the main men who swept Juventus to Serie A glory last season...

Angelo Peruzzi (Goalkeeper)
Italy's No.1 and you don't have to be a genius to work out why. Juventus conceded fewer goals than any other side in Serie A last term and much of that is down to Peruzzi. Yes, he's got a great defence in front of him, but similarly they know they've got a great 'keeper behind them.

Moreno Torricelli (Defender)
No-nonsense defender who takes no prisoners. He's big and tough, looks mean and plays meaner. But beneath the

Game

sell Roberto Baggio to AC Milan. Like Zidane, he was disappointing at Euro 96, but was back to his best last season and scored in the Champions' League against Manchester United and in the European Cup Final against Dortmund.

long flowing dark hair and the sneering looks, there lurks an excellent footballer. After all, you don't get to play for Juventus and Italy just because you're good at kicking people, do you?

Zinedine Zidane (Midfielder)

There were a few eyebrows raised when Juventus paid £3 million to take Zidane from Bordeaux two summers ago, particularly after his disappointing showing for France in Euro 96, but there are no question marks now. He had a stunning season and is well on his way to taking Michel Platini's mantle as Juve's favourite Frenchman.

Didier Deschamps (Midfielder)

Another French international midfielder, and not surprisingly he forms an all-conquering partnership with Zidane in the centre of the park. He might not be as elegant on the ball as his fellow countryman, but while Zidane might steal the headlines, he would be the first to admit that Deschamps deserves a large chunk of the credit.

Alessandro Del Piero (Striker)

The "boy wonder" who was so highly rated that Juve could

Christian Vieri (Striker)

The son of a famous footballing father, Bob, he grew up in Australia before returning 'home' to really make his mark. Had spells at several lower division sides before coming to the fore with Atalanta in 1995-96. That was enough to convince Juve and, although he was bought as one for the future, the 24-year-old more than played his part last term.and forced his way into the national team.

Nicola Amoruso (Striker)

Like Vieri, he was bought as a long-term replacement for either Vialli or Ravanelli, but injuries to Del Piero, Boksic and Padavano gave him his chance - alongside Vieri. Both took that chance and Amoruso, who scored 14 goals for relegated Padova in 1995-96, showed some real class. Such is their ability that Juve were confident enough to go into their European Cup Semi-Final against Ajax in Amsterdam with the two youngsters up front. Not surprisingly, they both scored in a 2-1 win.

Soccer Shocker

It was the night which rocked Italian football. And it was the night which signalled the end of an era. The venue was the San Siro Stadium, the home of AC Milan, the dominant Italian team of the last decade. Their visitors were Juventus and what followed sent shock waves through the whole of Europe. Juve simply crushed their hosts 6-1, with goals from Jugovic (two), Vieri (two), Zidane and Amoruso, but it was more than that...it was total humiliation.But what it proved is that Juventus are now head and shoulders above their rivals in the greatest League in Europe. It's up to the rest to try to catch them.We wish them luck...they'll need it!

Euro 97

Who are the top dogs across Europe?

While Juventus and Manchester United dominated in Italy and England, the other title winners in Europe were a mixture of great favourites and shock newcomers to the Champions scene. SHOOT explores Europe for the other number ones...

Germany - Bayern Munich

Bayern Munich lifted yet another Bundesliga title when they just kept ahead of Bayer Leverkusen.

Jurgen Klinsmann signed off in his homeland before moving to Sampdoria with another title-winning campaign but it was not a joyous one.

Internal rifts between the players led to several public arguments and it was player ability not team spirit that brought Bayern the title.

Bayer Leverkusen pushed them all the way, closing the gap to two points by the final whistle, with Borussia Dortmund, otherwise engaged in an amazing European Champions Cup triumph, coming with a late surge into third place.

With Christian Ziege joining Klinsmann in Italy at AC Milan and Markus Babbel also wanting out, Bayern may find it a tough mission to win the Bundesliga again, and impress in the Champions League.

Spain - Real Madrid

Not many people would be gutted if their club won the European Cup-Winners' Cup, reached their domestic Cup Final and finished second in the League with some of the most thrilling football at either end that you'll ever see. Oh, and beat your deadly rivals in a vital League match.

That's just what Bobby Robson's Barcelona did in 1996-97, but their fans had to swallow the bitterest of pills as Real Madrid kept the title in the capital, a year after Atletico won it.

The Primera Division was a two-horse race, with Barca and Real Madrid, inspired by Roberto Carlos (right), battling it out. Barca had Ronaldo in sensational form but they also had to contend with his off-the-field transfer speculation and the distraction of a hefty Cup schedule, brought about by success.

When Barca beat Paris St Germain in the European Cup-Winners' Cup Final in May, they had clawed themselves neck and neck with Real.

But while Ronaldo went off to spend the rest of the season playing for Brazil, Barca blew it three games from the end when they lost to lowly Hercules.

As Ronaldo left for Inter Milan and Bobby Robson considered his future, it was a sad end to a season when Barca scored around 120 goals in the season and conceded about 60.

Thrilling stuff....but not quite enough.

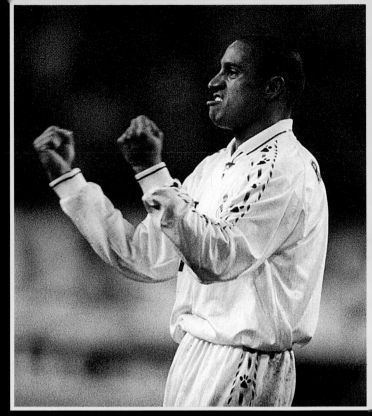

France - Monaco

What an astonishing season for Monaco! They cruised to the French Championship title, pushing PSG and Nantes into the chasing pack, and managed to reach the UEFA Cup Semi-Final. But, incredibly, only one Monaco player was in the France squad for Le Tournoi against Brazil, Italy and England...and that was goalie Fabien Barthez!

Ali Benarbia's wonderful form as an attacking midfielder should have earned him a call-up, especially as he kept Belgian ace Enzo Scifo out of the Monaco side.

Monaco did include Scotland's John Collins, who finally managed to win a Championship medal after six years of hell as Rangers beat his beloved Celtic to the title in Scotland, Brazilian ace Sonny Anderson and France's Thierry Henry.

These two took Newcastle apart in the UEFA Cup Quarter-Finals but were not enough to overcome mighty Inter Milan, who beat them 3-2 at the final hurdle.

18,000 watched the second-leg in Monte Carlo but only 4,000 returned to welcome the Champions for their last home game - can you imagine that at Old Trafford?

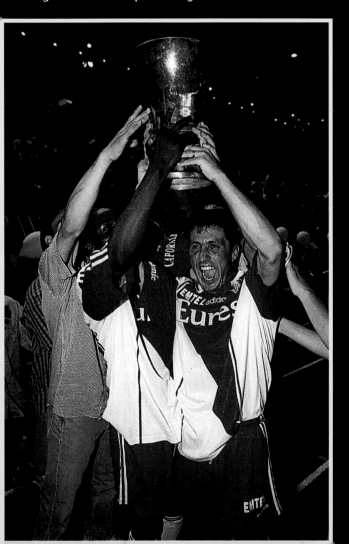

CHAMPS CAMP

The other 1996-97 title winners in Europe were;

Austria - **Austria Salzburg**
Belgium - **Lierse**
Bulgaria - **CSKA Sofia**
Croatia - **Croatia Zagreb**
Georgia - **Dynamo Tbilisi**
Netherlands - **PSV Eindhoven**
Portugal - **Porto**
Slovenia - **Maribor Branik**
Yugoslavia - **Partizan Belgrade**

Copa Load of This

The Copa America Tournament is the South American equivalent of the European Championship and is traditionally a feast of football. We all know about the likes of Maradona and Zico, but who are the new stars coming out of these countries?

Well, these will do for starters...

JUNINHO (Brazil)

The little Brazilian needs no introduction to English fans after his thrilling spell with Middlesbrough.

In two years on Teesside, Juninho won himself a permanent place in the hearts of English fans with his superb skills and fantastic attitude to the game. While Ravanelli whinged and whined, 'Juno' played the game with a smile on his face, even when things were going against him.

The 24-year-old, who cost Boro £4.75 million from Sao Paolo in October 1995, is already a major star but his fame could yet grow even more. With the World Cup looming in France next year the stage could be set for Juninho to prove himself as the world's greatest player.

He already wears the famous No.10 shirt for Brazil and looks more than capable of following the likes of Pele and Zico into footballing folklore.

RONALDO (Brazil)

Ronaldo is, quite simply, the best striker in the world at the moment. Yep, even better than Alan Shearer, he's that good!

He was voted FIFA's World Player of the Year last year and very few people would argue with that.

Certainly his coach in his time at Barcelona, former England manager Bobby Robson, agreed with that verdict.

He rates Ronaldo, 20, as the best player he has ever worked with and that is some compliment when you consider some of the talent Robson has had at his disposal during his long career, both in domestic and international football.

"Ronaldo is an amazing player with all the attributes that can keep him at the top of the game for a long time to come," says Robson.

"He has terrific pace, is very strong on the ball, hits the ball sweetly and has a very good eye for goal. There is nothing he can't achieve in the game."

Ronaldo leads the Brazilians into World Cup action in the summer of 1998 and is odds on to become the player of the tournament.

If Robson's comments are anything to go by - it might not be just one World Cup that he stars in.

ARIEL ORTEGA
(Argentina)

At just 23, Ortega is already rated as Argentina's best player since Diego Maradona.

A creative attacking midfielder with outstanding ball control, he carries a nation's hopes on his shoulders in much the same way as Maradona did. He was just 18 when he made his debut for River Plate and he has already won more than 30 caps for his country, for whom he is likely to star in the World Cup next year. Four years ago in America he spent much of the tournament on the substitutes' bench and only came into the team when Maradona was suspended for the last two matches. But he did enough in those games to show that Argentina could survive without their wayward captain, and he has been a regular ever since. He also set a new Argentinian transfer record in March 1997 when he quit River Plate to join Valencia in Spain for £7 million. Not surprisingly, he was an instant success.

MARCELO SALAS
(Chile)

An up and coming striker with a real eye for goal, Salas is an emerging star in South America.

He was an international by the time he was 20 and proved his class by finishing as top scorer in the Chilean First Division in 1995 as he helped Universidad de Chile win the Championship. But that brought him to the attention of bigger, more powerful clubs and, in 1996, Universidad reluctantly agreed to sell him to River Plate. The fee was £1.9 million - a sizeable investment in a player so young - and though Salas had to bide his time at River Plate because of their strong squad, he quickly became a favourite with the fans for his fearless and dangerous attacking, and of course his goals.

Injuries have interrupted his progress but he is now back to his best and looking to make his mark on the world game.

JAIME MORENO (Bolivia)

Remember him? He was a foreign signing at Middlesbrough even before the likes of Juninho and Ravanelli. His career never really got off the ground on Teesside though, and in two years at the club he made only a handful of appearances.

But there's no doubting his class as he has proved in America where he is now a major star with Washington DC United. He came to their attention in June 1996 when he played for Bolivia against the USA in Washington and scored a spectacular goal in only the second minute, racing 65 yards before finishing. DC United quickly snapped him up and he became a key player in their run to the Championship, and recognised as the leading striker in Major League Soccer.

At 20, he was a member of Bolivia's 1994 World Cup squad, and his pace, dribbling skills and artistry mark him out as a real star. However, he will probably need to move from America to truly be recognised as one.

GOAL-DEN BOY

Ronaldo's worth his weight in goals

Brilliant Brazilian Ronaldo is rated as the best - and most expensive - player in the world...and he more than proved his worth for Barcelona last season.

Although he couldn't help Barca snatch the Spanish title from Real Madrid, he still managed to finish the season streets ahead of his nearest rivals in the goal stakes.

The 20-year-old genius was Europe's leading goalscorer last term, plundering over 30 goals to take the Adidas Golden Shoe award ahead of fellow Brazilian Mario Jardel of Porto.

England skipper Alan Shearer was in the hunt too, ending his first season with Newcastle on 25 goals - an incredible achievement considering he missed so many games through injury.

Here's a check on the leading scorers around Europe last season:-

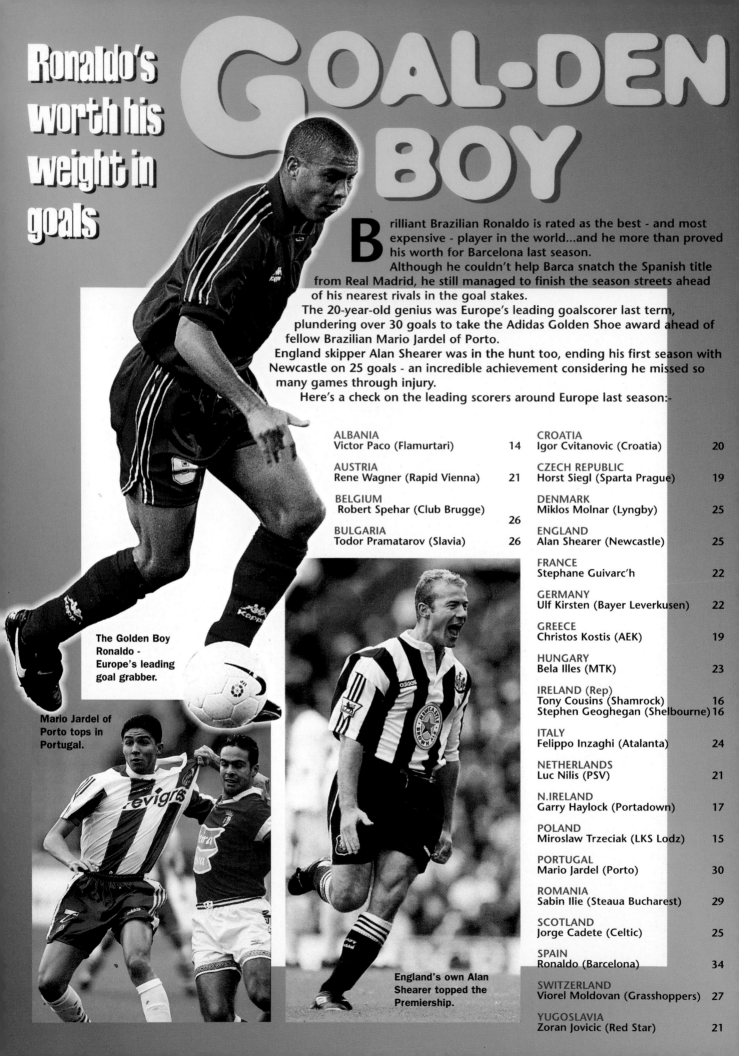

The Golden Boy Ronaldo - Europe's leading goal grabber.

Mario Jardel of Porto tops in Portugal.

England's own Alan Shearer topped the Premiership.

ALBANIA	
Victor Paco (Flamurtari)	14
AUSTRIA	
Rene Wagner (Rapid Vienna)	21
BELGIUM	
Robert Spehar (Club Brugge)	26
BULGARIA	
Todor Pramatarov (Slavia)	26
CROATIA	
Igor Cvitanovic (Croatia)	20
CZECH REPUBLIC	
Horst Siegl (Sparta Prague)	19
DENMARK	
Miklos Molnar (Lyngby)	25
ENGLAND	
Alan Shearer (Newcastle)	25
FRANCE	
Stephane Guivarc'h	22
GERMANY	
Ulf Kirsten (Bayer Leverkusen)	22
GREECE	
Christos Kostis (AEK)	19
HUNGARY	
Bela Illes (MTK)	23
IRELAND (Rep)	
Tony Cousins (Shamrock)	16
Stephen Geoghegan (Shelbourne)	16
ITALY	
Felippo Inzaghi (Atalanta)	24
NETHERLANDS	
Luc Nilis (PSV)	21
N.IRELAND	
Garry Haylock (Portadown)	17
POLAND	
Miroslaw Trzeciak (LKS Lodz)	15
PORTUGAL	
Mario Jardel (Porto)	30
ROMANIA	
Sabin Ilie (Steaua Bucharest)	29
SCOTLAND	
Jorge Cadete (Celtic)	25
SPAIN	
Ronaldo (Barcelona)	34
SWITZERLAND	
Viorel Moldovan (Grasshoppers)	27
YUGOSLAVIA	
Zoran Jovicic (Red Star)	21

YOUNG GUNS

Shooting To The Top

The stars of the Premiership used to be well-travelled, middle-aged, craggy veterans. Now they're fresh-faced, teenage, heart-throb kids who are more like pop stars from boy bands than footballers.

But that doesn't stop them taking the rough with the smooth on the footie pitch and coming out on top.

These boys are the future of the game - they're stars now, but just wait till the millenium when they'll be bigger than Barnes, faster than Ferdinand and sharper than Shearer.

Here come the young guns....

A Class Becks n' Hesk

When David Beckham thrashed in monster goal after monster goal last season, he was talked about as the most exciting player in the Premiership. To kick off the season with an astonishing 55 yard drive over Wimbledon's Neil Sullivan was amazing enough, but to follow it with a series of classic long-range strikes throughout the season was magnificent.

By the summer of '97, Beckham was almost guaranteed a place in England's starting line-up. He'd led Manchester United to a sec-

SHOOT Profile

DAVID BECKHAM
Born: May 2nd 1975 in Leytonstone, London
Clubs: Preston NE (loan), Manchester United
Position: Centre or right midfield
England honours: Youth (4 caps), Under-21 (9 caps) and Full caps

Pro debut: for Preston v Doncaster March 4th 1995
Club honours: Man United;
FA Youth Cup 1991-92, 92-93
FA Premiership 1995-96, 96-97
FA Cup 1995-96
Current value: £7 million

ond successive championship triumph and the semi-finals of the European Cup.

Young Player of the Year in 1997, Becks could do no wrong.

Then came England's World Cup qualifier in Poland. A 2-0 victory was greeted with joy, but Beckham struggled badly.

Suddenly people realsied what he was - a 22-year-old expected to play like an established international.

One below-par performance also made fans reflect on what incredible progress Becks has made in two years; from a loan spell at Preston to a regular place in the United line-up to a major star and England international. Oh, and he's going out with Posh Spice. Wow!

Now Becks is feared like a world star and will be under the pressure his United mate Ryan Giggs was under after his explosive start to his career. if he handles it half as well, Beckham will be beatin' 'em well into next century.

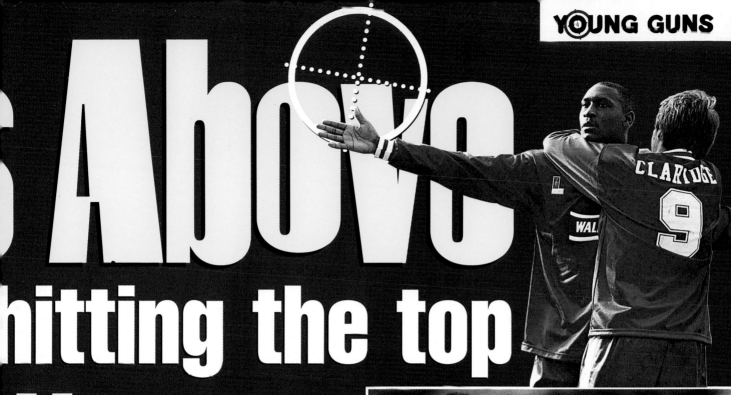

Above

hitting the top

He went to the same school as Gary Lineker and he plays up front for Leicester. That's all we knew about Emile Heskey when he first appeared in Leicester's line-up in 1995-96. But after a superb first season in the Premiership, Heskey is now one of the country's most wanted prospects.

if it wasn't for Leicester's remarkable form on their return to the top flight, Heskey would have been counting his money at Old Trafford, Anfield or Highbury. Instead, he played a major part in Leicester's shock top ten Premiership finish and trip to Europe after winning the Coca-Cola Cup.

By doing so well for City, his own form almost prevented him getting a big move. But homeboy Heskey is happy at Filbert Street and knows that if he continues to score and provide for the likes of Steve Claridge like he did last season, he'll be able to name his own price.

And what people keep forgetting is that he's only 19! His Leicester boss Martin O'Neill feared he'd burn out from playing too often, with Leicester and England Under-21s both desperate for his services. And while his explosive performances were less frequent towards the end of 1996-97, he still ran himself into the ground in the Coca-Cola Cup Final.

While winning the cup will be the highlight of the season for Leicester, anyone who saw it will never forget the goal he set up for Steve Calridge against Man United on the way to Wembley, backheeling the ball up while in mid-flight for Claridge to volley home. Stunning...but not surprsing after what we've seen so far from the Hesk.

SHOOT Profile

EMILE HESKEY
Born: January 11th 1978 in Leicester
Club: Leicester City
Position: Centre forward or right-wing
England honours: Youth and Under-21

(5 caps)
Pro debut: for Leicester at QPR March 8th 1995
Club honours: Leicester; First Division Play-Off winners 1996, Coca-Cola Cup Winners 1996-7
Current value: £4.5 million

When you think of a footballer called Hughes, it's normally Mark. And it's nearly always a Welsh player. But two young midfielders are trying to change that as Paul Hughes, Mark's team-mate at Chelsea, and Stephen Hughes, across London at Arsenal, are making names all for themselves...

The Hughe
Paul and Steve

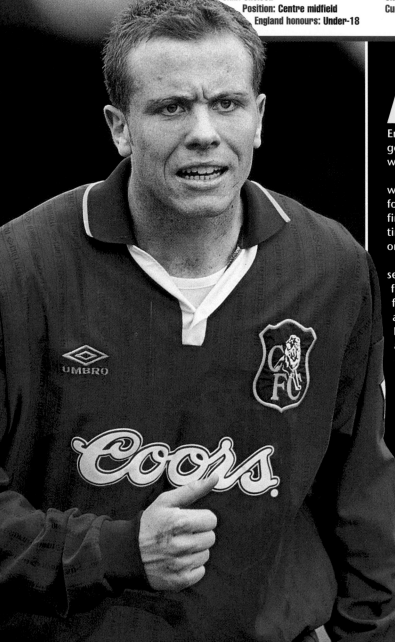

SHOOT Profile

PAUL HUGHES
Born: April 18th 1976 in Hammersmith
Club: Chelsea
Position: Centre midfield
England honours: Under-18

Schoolboys
Pro debut: for Chelsea v Derby January 18th 1997
Club honours: None
Current value: £3 million

At 17-years-old Paul Hughes was cruising through life, playing for Chelsea reserves, England boys and looking good for a cracking career with Glenn Hoddle's team.

Then things went horribly wrong and it was another four years before he was finally launched into the big time and he didn't half land on his feet.

After three years out with a series of awful injuries, Paul finally appeared in the Blues first team as a half-time sub against Derby last January. But this was no low-key arrival of another Hughes to confuse the Chelsea fans. This was the real thing.

Hughes played a lovely one-two with Roberto Di Matteo and slid the ball in for a crackin' debut goal! He held his place in the squad, either filling in at left wing-back or playing in his favoured central-midfield position, as Ruud Gullit shuffled his pack on the route to Wembley. Hughes was left out of the FA Cup Final side but he's got his own special memories of a stylish arrival on

the scene:

"I was nervous the night before my debut but when you're actually involved in the whole thing, your nerves just go," he told SHOOT. "I've been training with these people everyday and they know what I can do. It's just like going to work - but in front of 30,000 people!

"Some people freeze but no, I loved it. Rudi said: 'Hughesie, you're coming on' and I said 'Cheers, mate'! I was well chuffed with the goal. Things couldn't have gone any better unless I'd hit an overhead kick in from forty yards!"

"My injuries were disheartening and I did think 'Am I meant to be a footballer?' But I had to work really hard and you know what life's like without football. You don't take anything for granted. Knowing that the manager wants you to get fit so he can play you is what keeps you going. I deserve to have got here now and I'll enjoy it more. And I know that if I get another injury, I can deal with it."

Let's hope he never has to again. At this rate, the only thing he'll have to deal with is stardom.

s Brothers
et London alight

When Stephen Hughes made his Arsenal debut at Barnsley two years ago, he thought it was the start of something big. But then Bruce Rioch, the Arsenal boss then, sent him back to the reserves for a year. Arsene Wenger left him there and by Christmas last year, Hughesie was getting very frustrated.

" I was so down in the dumps. I thought it would be my season but I wasn't even training with the first team most of the time," he reveals. "I went to see the manager and said, 'What's happening? If I'm not part of your plans I want to move'. He said 'Bide your time and you'll get your chance'. And he's lived by his word: about three weeks after, I was in. Now everything's changed. I wake up in the morning and feel really happy!"

And so he should. He got his chance last season because of injuries to David Platt and Paul Merson, but his superb displays in central midfield, including a goal in the FA Cup win at Sunderland, meant he was

getting a game every week throughout the second-half of the season.

And that lead to a regular place in England Under-21s, to add to his schoolboy, Under-16 and Under-18 caps. Quite a career so far.

"It's been unbelievable. Since I got a chance, everything's gone great. My whole life's changed.

"There are no better players than Dennis Bergkamp and Ian Wright and you're playing with them every day. I used to be in awe of them but now I've got used to it."

Too right he has. And if his crafty left foot continues to cause havoc in opposition defences, the fans comparing him to Highbury legend Liam Brady may not be too far off the mark.

SHOOT Profile

STEPHEN HUGHES
Born: September 18th 1976 in Wokingham
Club: Arsenal
Position: Centre or left midfield
England honours: Schoolboys, Under-

16, Youth, Under-21 (4 caps)
Pro debut: for Arsenal at Barnsley (Coca-Cola Cup) October 24th 1995
Club honours: Arsenal;
FA Youth Cup 1993-94
Current value: £4 million

England is awash with talented teenagers and young guns establishing themselves at senior level. Some are in the Premiership, some aren't, but they're all targeted by the biggest clubs as the Tony Adams, Paul Ince and Alan Shearer of the Year 2000. Here's our run-down on a few more of the men, or boyz, to watch...

Rio Ferdinand

SHOOT Profile

RIO FERDINAND
Born: November 7th 1978 in east London
Club: West Ham United
Position: Centre-back
England honours: Youth and Under-21

(2 caps)
Pro debut: for West Ham v Sheffield Wed May 5th 1996
Club honours: West Ham; FA Youth Cup runners-up 1995-96
Current value: £4 million

When Alvin Martin left West Ham after 15 years at Upton Park, hammers fans wondered who would fill his boots. Big money was spent on centre-backs Marc Rieper, Slaven Bilic and Richard Hall but it was a teenager from West Ham's own youth team who emerged as their number one defender.

Rio Ferdinand was thrown into the team at 17 and put in some quality performances worthy of his classy name. Now Rio is fast closing on cousin Les Ferdinand in the England team.

Chris Perry

SHOOT Profile

CHRIS PERRY
Born: April 26th 1973 in Sutton
Club: Wimbledon
Position: Centre-back
England honours: None

Pro debut: for Wimbledon v Liverpool April 4th 1994
Club honours: None
Current value: £5 million

There are not many Wimbledon fans, but one of them is actually in the team! Chris Perry watched the Dons from the Plough Lane terraces in the eighties and the highlight of his life remains watching them win the FA Cup in 1988. Closest to that must be his super form last season in the Premiership when the 24-year-old helped the Dons to the edge of Europe with some fantastic displays.

Alex Ferguson is just one of his many fans and 5ft 8in Perry could go on to be the smallest centre-back to play for England!

Michael Branch

SHOOT Profile

MICHAEL BRANCH
Born: October 18th 1978 in Liverpool
Club: Everton
Position: Centre forward
England honours: Schoolboys, Under-

16, Youth, Under-21 caps
Pro debut: for Everton at Man United February 21st 1996
Club honours: None
Current value: £4 million

When team-mates and coaches say you'll be better than Robbie Fowler, you know you've got one amazing talent inside you. That's what Michael Branch has to live with, but he should deal with the pressure.

He scored freely at junior level, but his first Premiership season brought few goals, despite fine displays.

If the goals start flying in at Goodison in '98, you can be sure Branch will become a striker to match Fowler's feats across Stanley Park.

Team For 2000

Here's a line-up of the most-promising young players queuing up for a place in the full England team:

(GOALIE)
Richard Wright
Ipswich

(DEFENCE RIGHT TO LEFT)
Riccardo Scimeca
Aston Villa
Rio Ferdinand
West Ham
Chris Perry
Wimbledon

(MIDFIELD RIGHT TO LEFT)
Matthew Oakley
Southampton
Jamie Carragher
Liverpool
Jody Morris
Chelsea
Danny Murphy
Crewe
Danny Granville
Chelsea

(STRIKERS)
Michael Branch
Everton
Michael Owen
Liverpool

WINNERS
THEY'RE ALL TOP CLASS!

Chelsea's Dennis Wise proudly displays the FA Cup

United made it four Premiership titles out of five

Rangers made it nine titles in a row in Scotland

Bobby Robson steered Barcelona to the Cup-Winners' Cup

Super Al was the Premiership's top scorer...again

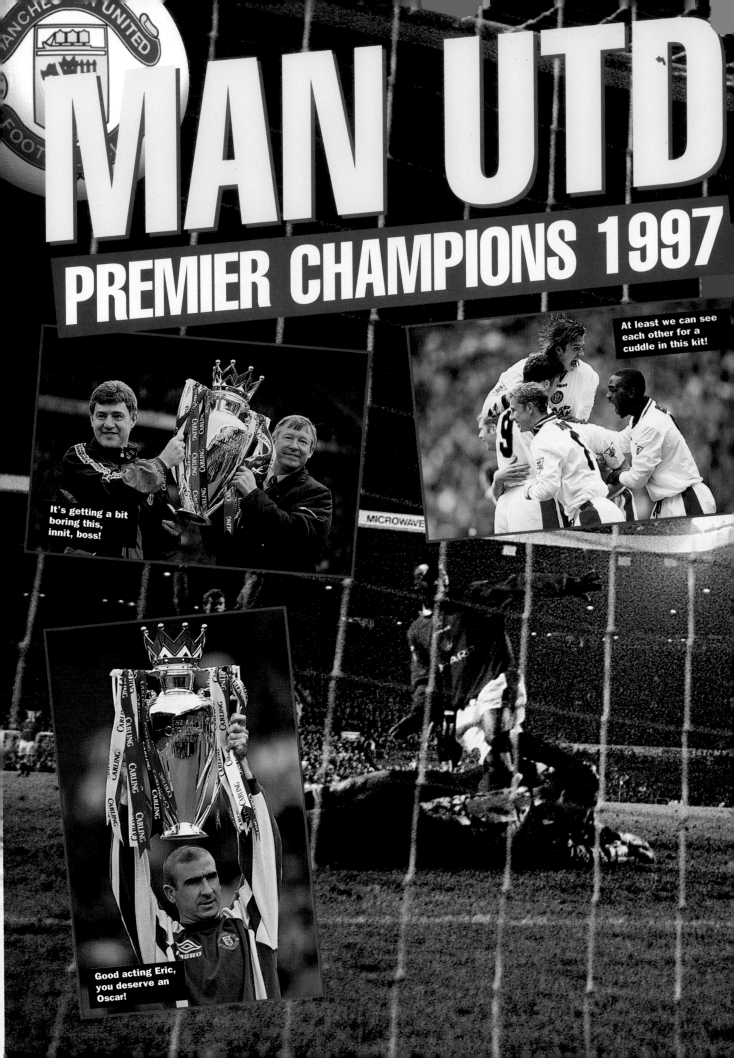

MAN UTD

PREMIER CHAMPIONS 1997

It's getting a bit boring this, innit, boss!

At least we can see each other for a cuddle in this kit!

Good acting Eric, you deserve an Oscar!

Sign of the times: Celtic suffer at Rangers' hands again

Walter works as Rangers boss Smith holds aloft the Cup again

RANGERS
SCOTS PREMIER CHAMPIONS 1997

Can we keep this nice white board as well please, boss?

BELL'S WINNERS SEASON

CHELSEA

FA CUP WINNERS 1997

Chelsea's happy chappies parade the Cup

Steady Eddie Newton scores the second goal to seal the Cup

Blue is the colour...success is the game

The Ruud boy grabs his first trophy in England

KILMARNOCK

SCOTTISH CUP WINNERS 1997

TENNENT'S
LAGER

EXIT 11

SCOTTISH CUP

TENNENTS

**Water carry on:
The celebrations
start to spill over**

Wright On: Paul Wright wins the Cup for Killie

SCOTTISH CUP

Falkirk took a tumble as Killie claimed the Cup

Captain Jim McIntyre gleefully lofts the Cup

LEICESTER

COCA-COLA CUP WINNERS 1997

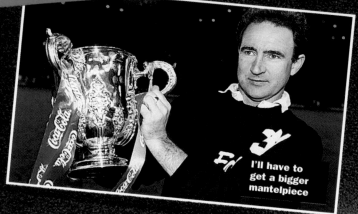

I'll have to get a bigger mantelpiece

Okay, who let the bear join the team group?

THE Coca-Cola CUP 1997 WINNERS

Scoring the winner has gone to Steve Claridge's head

Ally McCoist proves deadly from three inches against Hearts in the Final

Shock horror - Rangers have won another trophy

RANGERS
SCOTS COCA-COLA CUP WINNERS 1997

BOLTON
DIVISION ONE CHAMPIONS 1997

Gerry Taggart and Gudni Bergsson in celebratory mood

Keith Branagan gives Alan Thompson a lift all the way to the Premiership

CONGRATULATIONS FROM Nationwide

BURY

DIVISION TWO CHAMPIONS 1997

CONGRATULATIONS FROM Nationwide

smiths wigan THE WIGAN BEER COMPANY PORT PETROLEUM Sonsico JJB SPORTS PUMA PUMA TILBURY DOUGLAS

CONGRATULATIONS FROM Nationwide

WIGAN

DIVISION THREE CHAMPIONS 1997

BORUSSIA DORTMUND
EUROPEAN CUP WINNERS 1997

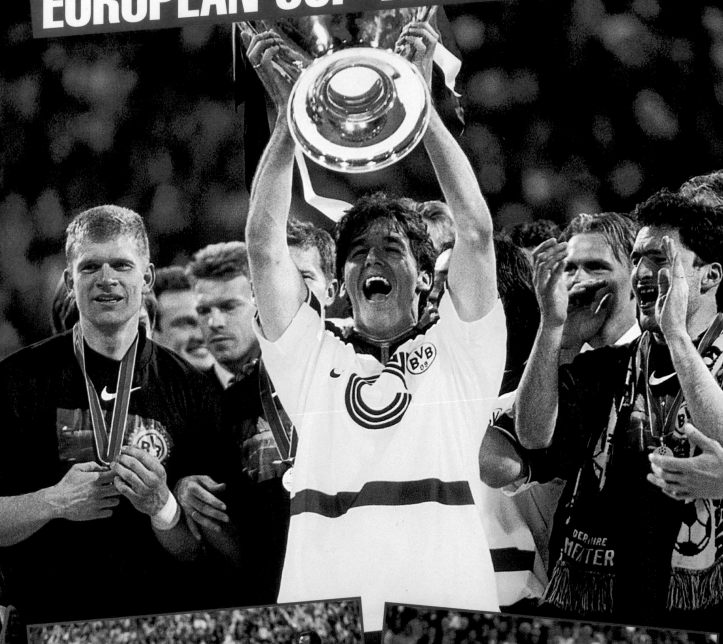

Karlheinz Riedle celebrates one of his two goals against Juventus

Lars Ricken gives Dortmund the Cup with the third goal in their 3-1 win over Juve

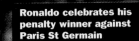

BARCELONA
EUROPEAN CUP-WINNERS' CUP WINNERS 1997

SCHALKE 04
UEFA CUP WINNERS 1997

Olaf Thon holds aloft the UEFA Cup

THE GOLDEN
Top League scorers

Shearer strikes against Sunderland

....and then against Forest

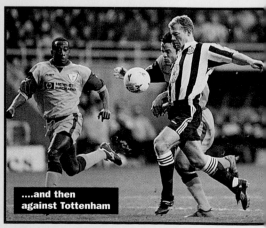

....and then against Tottenham

25 GOALS **ALAN SHEARER** Newcastle

BOYS 1996/97

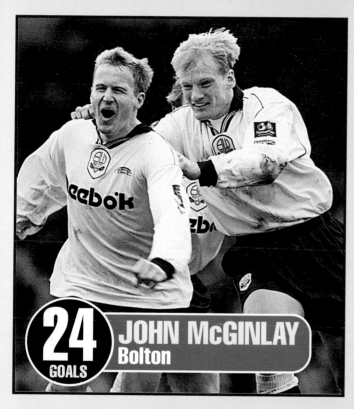

24 GOALS — JOHN McGINLAY Bolton

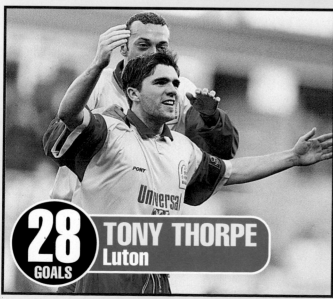

28 GOALS — TONY THORPE Luton

31 GOALS — GRAEME JONES Wigan

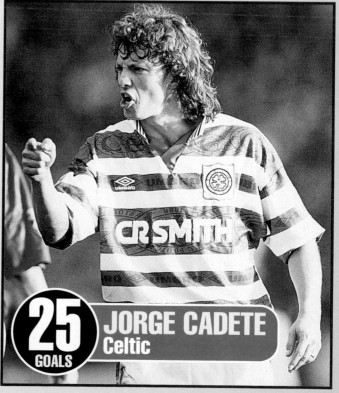

25 GOALS — JORGE CADETE Celtic

RIO FERDINAND
WEST HAM
SHOOT

Great Scots

No great surprise in the Scottish Premier last season - but who'd have put their hard-earned sheckles on Falkirk and Kilmarnock battling it out in the Final of the Scottish Cup?

Predictably, it was Rangers who ran away with the Premiership title - a record equalling ninth League success on the trot - as Celtic's own title bid faltered.

With the Ibrox giants continuing to shell out fortunes on even more foreign imports, it's difficult to imagine any Scottish club, Celtic included, ending the Gers domination north of the border.

It can't be long before Rangers' over-whelming success in their own country is rewarded with a place in the impending European Super League.

Two teams unlikely to be in such an exalted position are Kilmarnock and Falkirk, but there was no denying their moment of triumph when they walked out for the Scottish Cup Final last May - the Killies winning by the odd goal.

More Scottish news to follow over the next few pages.......

Jubilant Rangers ace striker Ally McCoist (left) celebrates another Scottish Premier Championship title and Kilmarnock captain Ron Montgomerie displays the Scottish Cup after their 1-0 win over Falkirk in the Final.

United Nations

Spotlight on Rangers' fab foreigners

RANGERS have transformed their team into a United Nations X1 to chase European glory.

A Scottish accent is rare these days in the Ibrox dressing-room...... because it is filled wall to wall with foreign stars.

The Champions have more than a full team of continental players on their books as they chase their 10th League title on the trot.

And now chairman David Murray insists he will break the bank to grab glory in the Champions League.

The Rangers owner failed with a massive £19 million bid to lure Brazilian striker Ronaldo to Glasgow from Barcelona but did succeed in taking Italian ace Sergio Porrini to Ibrox.

The Gers faithful, now more than ever, can still feast their eyes on a galaxy of stars this season.

Italian ace Lorenzo Amoruso has taken over from departed captain Richard

Having a team of international all-stars does have its drawbacks, however.

Manager Walter Smith's biggest headache is giving pre match team talks to his United Nations line up.

But he insists there is no jealously among the ranks of home based players which include super striker Ally McCoist and Gordon Durie.

"Signing the best players to perform for Rangers has always been our number one objective," he says..

"The players are all professionals and everyone knows they have a part to play."

Gough at the heart of the defence. The Fiorentina star turned his back on a megabucks move to Manchester United infavour of Ibrox.

Amoruso admits: "Not many players turn down a move to Old Trafford. But once I spoke to Rangers I knew I had to play for them.

"The chairman, David Murray, made it clear that I was under no obligation to sign even though we had agreed verbally. But I liked the way he worked."

A weekly wage of £12,000 obviously helped Amoruso make his decision as well!

Italian ace Amoruso has been joined in the Ibrox defence by Norwegian STALE STENSAAS and Aussie TONY VIDMAR, who has replaced home grown left-back David Robertson who has joined Leeds.

Swedish ace JONAS THERN is now rubbing shoulders with Paul Gascoigne in midfield. And up front Italian youngster RINO GATUSO was snatched on a free transfer to join Chilean ace SEBASTIAN ROZENTAL.

Rozental barely kicked a ball for Rangers last season before picking up a serious leg injury but he is now back on song.

Swede JOCKY BJORKLAND, Yugoslav GORDAN PETRIC and German JORG ALBERTZ make up the Ibrox all star line up with Dutchman PETER VAN VOSSEN and Danish beanpole ERIK BO ANDERSEN.

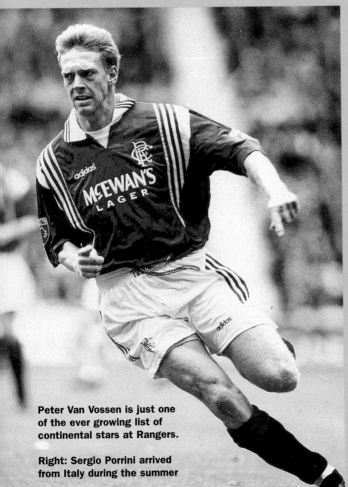

Peter Van Vossen is just one of the ever growing list of continental stars at Rangers.

Right: Sergio Porrini arrived from Italy during the summer

Jorg
Albertz
RANGERS

Alan
Stubbs
CELTIC

Celtic:

Things can only get better

says Alan Stubbs

CELTIC fans thought things could only get better when they saw Rangers equal their coveted nine in a row record.

But they were forced to look back in anger as paradise was engulfed in crisis.

Foreign strikers Paolo di Canio and Jorge Cadete begged to leave the club after cash wrangles.

And Celtic were left hunting a manager after Tommy Burns was sacked.

The writing was on the wall for beleaguered Burns after the Bhoys crashed to a sensational Scottish Cup Semi Final defeat by minnows Falkirk.

Less than a month later he was axed from the hottest seat in Scottish football.

But record signing Alan Stubbs has promised Celtic fans they can put their troubles behind them and prepare for a party next May.

The £4 million defender is desperate to silence the critics who wrote him off as a flop last season.

Stubbs admits the huge price tag placed on him by the move from Bolton weighed heavily on his mind.

"For one reason or another things didn't work out last season," he says.

"But all that matters now is that we stop Rangers taking their success any further - and I believe we can do that as a team.

"We lost the League last time because of four defeats by Rangers and in each game we were desperately unlucky.

"The bottom line is that we are not too far behind the club on the other side of Glasgow."

Stubbs insists Rangers' all star line up holds no fears for him.

"A lot of people have asked me what I think about all the players Rangers have been signing.

"They are all quality players but Rangers will still have to gel together as a team after the loss of Richard Gough and David Robertson. Everyone knows Gough was the key man in the heart of the defence.

"It is important that Celtic players believe in their own ability. We must match fire with fire."

Celtic on the other hand will have to gel together BEHIND the scenes after washing their dirty linen in public last season.

Dutch striker Pierre van Hooijdonk left to join Nottingham Forest after failing to cash in on a gentleman's agreement with Fergus McCann.

And Portugese strike Jorge Cadete and Italian winger Paulo di Canio both insisted that they too were being hung out to dry.

Celtic's Jorge Cadete was top scorer in Scotland last season but his future at Parkhead became clouded at the end of the campaign

A-Z
Who's who north of the border?

Scotland boss Craig Brown.

A is for Lorenzo AMORUSO. The rugged Italian has brought some style to the Rangers defence since his £3.95 million signing in the summer. Well, at £12,000 a week he can afford Armani shades!

B is for BROWN. Craig Brown wasn't the popular choice as Scotland boss but he has few critics now with the Scots on the verge of reaching next year's World Cup finals in France.

C is for Jorge CADETE. The Portuguese striker certainly banged in goals for Celtic - 25 in the League alone - and became a firm favourite with the Parkhead fans, but it wasn't enough to halt The Gers.

D is for DRUGS. Hearts striker Stefan Paille brought shame on the club when he received a FIFA ban for taking a banned stimulant which enhances performance.

E is for ESTONIA who refused to turn up for the kick-off in the World Cup-tie in Tallin against Scotland as a protest against the kick-off being moved.

F is for FERGUS McCann. The little guy with the terrible taste in bonnets must pull something out of the hat for frustrated Celtic fans following the end-of-season turmoil.

G is for GAZZA. The English ace still has his troubles on and off the park but he admits he is hooked on Scotland for fishing.

H is for HEART-BREAK as Hearts lost the Coca-Cola Cup Final Rangers after a six-goal thriller.

Celtic's Jorge Cadete.

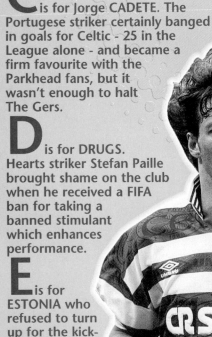

I is for ILIAN Kiriakov. Aberdeen fans thought the Bulgarian midfield ace was the man for the job but he sounds more like the Man from Uncle.

Ilian Kiriakov.

J is for Darren JACKSON. It's been a case of better late than never for the Hibs striker who is now a red hot favourite with Scotland fans. Jacko has also become a model pro as a part time model.

K is for KILMARNOCK. The Ayrshire club shocked everyone by winning the Scottish Cup last season. But the reaction of potential European Cup-Winners' Cup opponents was Kil Who?

L is for LUGGY. That's the nickname unfortunate St Johnstone boss Paul Sturrock has been forced to lug around during his career. One look at his ears will tell you why Saints could lift a Cup this season.

Easy World Cup points for Scotland in Estonia - well nearly!

V is for Pierre VAN Hooijdonk who swapped Celtic for a dream move to Nottingham Forest just two months before they dropped out of the Premiership.

W is for WONDERBOY Paul Lambert who lifted the European Cup with German cracks Borussia Dortmund less than 12 months after leaving Motherwell to try his luck on the continent.

M is for MAMA MIA. That was the reaction of Celtic's volatile Italian winger Paolo di Canio when the club refused his request for a loadsalira extension to his contract at Parkhead.

N is for NIGHTMARE. Celtic's record £4 million signing Alan Stubbs is hoping for no more sleepless nights after a season wrecked by injury.

O is for OWEN Coyle who won Motherwell's player of the year award after only four months at the club. Doesn't say much for the rest of them!

P is for PITTODRIE. The home of Aberdeen was like a morgue last season after a dismal season which prompted calls for boss Roy Aitken to be axed.

Q is for QUEENS Park Rangers flop Mark Hateley who was brought back to Rangers for the title showdown with Celtic and promptly got himself sent-off.....some help you were Mark!

R is for early RETIREMENT. Celtic captain Paul McStay was forced to hang up his boots prematurely at the age of 32 because of an severe ankle injury.

S is for SUPER Ally McCoist. The Rangers pin up and record goalscorer will spend more time flogging strips than flogging himself to death on the park after working out a deal which will groom him as a future commercial boss of the club.

T is for TEN in a row. Celtic fans will be literally green with envy if Rangers can set clinch a record breaking tenth League title on the trot this season.

U is for ULSTERMAN Danny Griffin who turned down a move from St Jonhstone to Premiership new boys Derby. Is that loyalty or what?

X is for XTRAORDINDARY. Cup shock troops Falkirk pulled off the giantkilling feat of the season with the help of their very own giant, 6ft 7in defender Kevin James before losing to KIllie in the Cup Final.

Y is for YANKEE doodle dandy Richard Gough who left Rangers for a few dollars more to move across the Atlantic and play with Kansas City Whizz.

Z for zzzzzzzzzzzzzzzzz......the sound which was heard as Raith Rovers slipped through the relegation trap door.

Mark Hateley (left) and Darren Jackson (right).

Paul Lambert lifts the European Cup.

Stewart Kerr

Greg Shields

Robbie Winters

Danny Griffin

David Weir

STEWART KERR (Celtic)

The former Scotland Under-21 'keeper looks certain to earn a full cap this season. This young boxing fanatic has made the number one spot his own at Parkhead after taking over from Gordon Marshall. Kept Celtic's season alive last term with a string of stunning displays which earned him rave reviews.

Shoot rating: 8/10.

DANNY GRIFFIN (St Johnstone)

Derby boss Jim Smith should know all about this youngster - he's tried to buy him twice. Smith had to look elsewhere when the 20-year-old decided to stick with Premier League new boys St Johnstone to sign a new two-year deal. But central defender Griffin has more experience than most having earned a handful of full caps with Northern Ireland.

Shoot rating: 9/10

GREG SHIELDS (Rangers)

Greg would be a first team regular at any other club in the country. The 21-year-old starred for Rangers in the European Cup run last season covering for injured stars. He even scored a wonder goal in a friendly against Ajax at the Amsterdam Arena. But the stong defender has been forced to wait patiently in the reserves while gaffer Walter Smith sticks with the big-name buys.

Shoot rating: 8/10

ROBBIE WINTERS (Dundee United)

Winters is one of the fastest players in the country. The 22-year-old's lightning pace terrorised defenders throughout last season. Scots boss Craig Brown is a big fan of the winger but has yet to give him a cap call. Has been linked with several moves south but United boss Tommy McLean is reluctant to let him go.

Shoot rating: 9/10

DAVID WEIR (Hearts)

This could be the year that sees David Weir break into the big-time. Signed by Hearts from Falkirk a year ago the 27-year-old was a rock in the Jambos defence throughout last season. That prompted Scots boss Craig Brown to hand him his international debut against Wales in May.

Shoot rating: 8/10

the Scots

Young guns heading for glory

David Bagen

Martin Baker

Charlie Miller

DAVID BAGEN (Kilmarnock)

The scruffy little winger was the star in Killie's Scottish Cup glory trail last season. His old-fashioned attacking style has made him a massive hit at Rugby Park. Under-21 boss Tommy Craig is just one of his fans and Bagen has been included in the past few squads. He will have to be one of Killie's major players as they search for more silverw are in the Cup Winners' Cup.

Shoot rating: 9/10

David Rowson

SIMON DONNELLY (Celtic)

Sid was tipped as the new Kenny Dalglish whe he broke onto the scene two years ago. However, the 22-year-old's form dipped as he found it difficult to shift the club's star names from the Parkhead dream team. National boss Craig Brown gave him a shock cap call against Wales last May as a second-half substitute.

Shoot rating: 8/10

Simon Donnelly

CHARLIE MILLER (Rangers)

Off the field problems and injury have limited Charlie's appearances in a Rangers shirt. He then looked to have got his act together before a broken arm forced him out for two months.
Still an exciting creative midfielder who has formed a good relationship with Gazza. The 21-year-old was a regular in the Under-21 side from his early teens.

Shoot rating: 8/10

MARTIN BAKER (Kilmarnock)

The 22-year-old left-back has finally got his chance of playing in the Premier League. Seven Under-21 caps while at First Division St Mirren prompted Killie to make a move taking him to Rugby Park in the summer. The former bad-boy has been sent-off three times in one season - mostly for dissent - but has since cleaned up his act.

Shoot rating: 9/10

DAVID ROWSON (Aberdeen)

Another former Scotland Under-21 skipper who grasped his chance with both hands. Took over from crocked midfielder Paul Bernard at the start of last season and hasn't left the side. His tough tackling and forward running have made him a hit with the Pittodrie supporters. But Scots boss Craig Brown has yet to give the 22-year-old a full international cap.

Shoot rating: 8/10

BELL'S PLAYER OF THE YEAR 1997

BRIAN LAUDRUP
RANGERS

SHOOT

SHOOT

Eat football, breathe football, read SHOOT – just like the stars

SHOOT: On sale every Tuesday
STILL BRITAIN'S FAVOURITE FOOTIE WEEKLY

CROSSWORD ANSWERS

Crossword answers
Across: 1. Gianfranco Zola. 10. Neville. 11. Barcelona. 12. Lange. 13 and 14 across. De Agostini. 16. Castle. 17. Lazio. 18. Lee. 20. Petric. 22. Adams. 23. Lupescu. 27. Canada. 28 and 6 down. Real Zaragoza. 29. Metz. 33. Stag. 36. Neeskens. 37. Tel. 39. Nadal. 40. Teammate.

Down: 1. Ginola. 2. Alvin Martin. 3. Filbert. 4. Aberdeen. 5. Cuba. 7. Leeds Road. 8. Boli. 9. Mariner. 15. Clyde. 18. Lambert. 19. Spackman. 21. Clark. 22. Australia. 24. Plan. 25. Save. 26. Flag. 30. Tweed. 32 and 38 across. Ian St John. 34. Ashby. 35. Skol. 37. Tom. 38 and 31 across. Joe Kinnear.

SCOTTISH PREMIER DIVISION CHAMPIONS 1996/7

Glasgow

SHOOT ANNUAL is published by IPC Magazines Ltd., Specialist Group, 24th Floor, King's Reach Tower, Stamford Street, London SE1 9LS. SHOOT ANNUAL must not be sold at more than the recommended selling price as shown on the cover. All rights reservered and reproduction without permission is strickly forbidden. Finishing & Binding: Butler & Tanner Ltd., 35 Headfort Place, Belgravia, London SW1X 7DE. Text Printers: Southernprint Web Offset Ltd., 17-19 Factory Road, Upton Industrial Estate, Poole, Dorset, BH16 5SN. Cover Printers: CSM Impact Litho Ltd., Units L1/L2 Grafton Way, West Ham Industrial Estate, Basingstoke, Hants RG22 6HY. Repro: Litho Origination Group PLC, 90/92 Pentonville Road, London N1 9HS.

BE PREMIER